'This book will he
an award v

**Tony Robinson OBE, The Micro Business Champion
and Co-Founder #MicroBizMatters**

HOW TO **WIN**
BUSINESS AWARDS

DENISE O'LEARY

WINNER

First published in 2020 by

Panoma Press Ltd
48 St Vincent Drive, St Albans, Herts, AL1 5SJ, UK
info@panomapress.com
www.panomapress.com

Book layout by Neil Coe.

978-1-784529-03-1

The right of Denise O'Leary to be identified as the author of this work has been asserted in accordance with sections 77 and 78 of the Copyright, Designs and Patents Act 1988.

A CIP catalogue record for this book is available from the British Library.

This book is available online and in bookstores.

Dedication

To my husband Malc and my sister Tracey, with love and gratitude for all of your support.

To my nieces Taylor and Scarlett – fulfil your dreams, you can be anything you want to be.

For Mum and Dad x

Testimonials

"Denise has spent her career helping businesses win – entrepreneurs will hugely benefit from her award-winning insight."

**Emma Jones MBE,
Founder – Enterprise Nation**

"Want to win? Read this! I'm a fan and judge of business awards and know the benefits they bring – this book will help you become an award winner."

**Tony Robinson OBE,
The Micro Business Champion and
Co-Founder #MicroBizMatters**

"This book is a must-have for anyone wanting to win awards."

**Debbie Gilbert,
Founder – Best Business Women Awards**

"Entering awards should form part of your marketing budget."

**Wilfred Emmanuel-Jones,
Founder – The Black Farmer**

"Don't let the blonde hair and purple exterior fool you! Denise O'Leary is a force to be reckoned with when it comes to all things marketing, award entries and bid writing. Having risen to the top ranks in the manufacturing and construction sectors, her knowledge is immense. If you are looking to win awards and improve your marketing, then Denise is the lady for you."

Alison Edgar,
The Entrepreneur's Godmother

"I loved your talk on how to win awards! This is the talk of the office today!"

Lara Barnes,
Wiltshire Women in Business Event

"Thrilled to have you Denise – and all the inspirational female force – with us at the Women in Construction seminar series today! #BIG5EXHIBITION"

Big 5 Expo, Dubai

Acknowledgments

To all those brave enough to have started your own business — I applaud you and your support network. Writing a book is like a focused marketing campaign — thanks to everyone who has inspired, supported and contributed to the content.

The book I wanted to create demanded several different perspectives, from people who were all esteemed business professionals, including award winners, judges, and those who run award ceremonies. It is with huge gratitude that I acknowledge the amazing contributions of Debbie Gilbert, founder of the Best Business Women Awards; Alec Jones-Hall, founder of the Thames Valley/South West Business and Community Awards; and Anita Jaynes, founder of the Business Exchange and 'The Techies'. Thanks also to Emma Jones MBE, founder of Enterprise Nation; Francesca James, co-founder of the Great British Entrepreneur Awards; Tony Robinson OBE of the #MicroBizMatters movement; and Gavan Wall. Your inputs were greatly appreciated.

Much appreciation to my friends Jan de Jonge for his business psychology expertise, Fiona Scott for her PR insight, and Taz Thornton for her epic awards ceremony story.

I am also indebted to all the past award winners who have shared the joy of their triumphs alongside their top tips so that others can win as well, these include Caroline Sparks and Gaby Lixton from Turtle Tots; Roni Savage of Jomas Associates; Wilfred Emmanuel-Jones, founder of The Black Farmer; and Julianne Ponan of Creative Nature.

Also a shoutout to Abi Purser, Adeem Younis, Alison Edgar, Angela Hughes, Angela Hicks, Anna Rabin, Catherine Gladwyn, Darren Clark, James Eades, Jo Macfarlane, Julie Grimes, Laura Birrell, Lynn Stanier, Natasha Penny, Rachel Spratling, Ray Dawson,

Sam Bramley, Sam Gooding, Simon Crowther, Simon Buck, Tracey Smolinski and Wendy Griffith.

Thanks to Mindy Gibbins-Klein and her team at Panoma Press for making this book a reality.

To the entire Purpol Marketing family of staff, and interns, past and present – thank you all for your amazing support.

Foreword

In 2012 I sat at the back of a huge ballroom in a lovely hotel attending my first awards ceremony. This was not the first awards I had entered, but it was the first one I had been selected as a finalist for. In my heart, I thought, I can't have won as they wouldn't have sat me here!

This was new territory for me. I had been in business for 14 years and entering awards had never occurred to me. A business associate suggested I should. The first time I entered, I didn't get through to the finals. Getting the rejection letter was horrible. I felt I wasn't good enough after all. Now I was despondent so pushed all thoughts of awards to the back of my mind.

Then at a networking event, I met another businesswoman who specialised in writing award entries. She told me to try again and enter a different award programme. I sent her my rejected entry. The pages of comments were a real eye-opener. I realised I hadn't communicated my achievements, showcased my passion and sent enough evidence to back up what I had shared in my entry. So, with her guidance, I worked on the entry. This not only got me to the finals, but to my surprise, it got me the winning trophy!

From the back of that ballroom I walked to the stage, applause all around me and collected my award. The feeling of pride was indescribable. A panel of independent judges had deemed me the best business against my competitors in that category. That was a pivotal moment in my business journey.

I gained so much from that first win. PR, new business, and a bug for awards that led me to win six more. This drove me to start the Best Business Women Awards. This is where I met Denise. She was a finalist in 2017 and went on to win in 2018. She never let being a finalist stop her from entering again! We have recognised over

300 women. Many have got some great publicity and new clients as a result, as well as enjoying a great night at the final!

In my opinion, there is nothing negative about entering awards. The information you need to gather and the questions you need to answer lead you to discover things about your business. This is such a valuable exercise. It may lead to new innovations and greater brand visibility.

Denise has written this book to help you find your way through the maze of entering awards. This will give you all the information you need to share with the judges to ensure you get to the finals. Winning awards is never easy. Rarely are they 'fixed'. Most award programmes are very credible and the judging process fair. You do of course need business success to enter!

There is a skill in writing an award entry. But it's not about being a great writer. It is simply about answering the questions and providing the evidence to enhance your entry. You need to communicate your passion and make the judges fall in love with your business. Make sure you carefully read the sections in this book on what to include and on what the judges hate! Go to this section first!

If I had given up and thrown in my awards towel after being rejected the first time, I would not be where I am now. I knew in my heart I had achievements worth sharing. Drawing a line under my first attempt was the best thing I did. Getting advice was the second-best thing I did. I wish this book had existed then.

Awards come under your marketing budget and should be in the marketing plan of every single business. Because the exposure you gain will get you more customers. Plus, it creates a buzz around you and your business. People love to work with an award-winning company. Awards create confidence and trust. Knowing a business has been validated by an external panel elevates you as an expert in your industry and gives you an advantage among your competitors.

Awards allow you to share success with your team, to recognise your staff and help in attracting new talent too.

I was delighted to be asked by Denise to contribute my advice for this book. Over the past five years I have seen the very worst entries to the very best. The worst simply did not follow the clear process required to succeed. So use the insights in this book to ensure that you do.

Now you know the benefits of being an award winner, there is no better person than Denise O'Leary to teach you the skills of where to find awards, what to include on the entry form and how to take home the trophy. She is sharing the knowledge gained from her bid writing and marketing career and her immense experience gained by being a multi-award winner herself.

I highly recommend this book for all business owners, managers and entrepreneurs who want to win awards. This is an invaluable resource.

I look forward to toasting your success at the winner's table!

Debbie Gilbert

Contents

Introduction

Many business owners and small businesses dream of the profile they could create and look on in admiration at other award winners. They wonder how they can achieve that success for themselves and their business.

WINNER – How to Win Business Awards has been written by multi-award winner Denise O'Leary who, as her day job, helps her clients win major bids and pitches.

Lack of confidence is an often-cited problem for small businesses alongside limited time and resources. They are keen to understand what benefits will be derived from winning awards, based on tips from prior winners and judges and, just as importantly, they also need to know what to avoid.

The process for winning awards is very similar to Denise's proven formula for winning bids – each award entry needs to be treated as a bespoke marketing campaign.

In easy to understand chapters, the book takes the potential award winner on a journey to success. Starting from "Has My Company Got What It Takes to Win an Award", right through to "How to Make Your Entry Stand Out" and ultimately what you can expect from an awards event with the "Tales From the Ceremony."

We include real life tips from winners and what they have included with their entries in order to get winning appeal. Also important are the hints from awards judges as to what they look for when assessing an entry, what they award points to, and also what they don't like to see. All stages of the process are explained and then supported with Top Tip graphics to summarise the learning. This is fully reinforced by exercises for the reader to capture key aspects of their business story as they progress, making entry in the future so much easier.

The book has additional insights from a business psychologist on why award entry can provide validation for yourself and your business. He explains the influence of the individual's attitude to risk, how to exploit the personality traits of a winner, and how the psychological process of entry can improve your attitude toward your business to drive further success.

A summary chapter is also presented at the end of the book. It acts as a practical reminder when the reader is in the actual entry process, covering all of the elements to be considered.

The content of this book is designed for universal appeal and application for business awards, as well as grant applications and bids. All the useful advice is in one place and designed for reference regardless of the type of award you want to win.

The learning is reinforced with key exercises to get the reader to consider how they apply the process to their own business. It is completed as they progress building the story of their business to aid in future entry completion.

Case studies are included in the way of tips from past winners, judges, and those who actually run awards. These insightful stories bring the awards journey to life and present real-life proven examples of what to include to make your entry a winner.

Is it time for your business to receive some recognition?

Do you want to *win* awards and promote your business?

Read on and we will help you get that amazing accolade.

The World of Business Awards

There you are, hearing the shortlist read out, pulse quickening, heart racing. Your name is on the big screen alongside the other finalists. Then the sponsor unveils the gilded envelope and starts to read out the characteristics of the winner. By now your pulse is ringing in your ears – were those phrases related to me? And finally, the big reveal – *you have won!* Your name is in lights, your photo is shown to the entire room, and the space erupts in applause as you quickly come to your senses and realise you have to move toward the stage to collect your magnificent prize.

Is this the feeling that you dream of? Or perhaps you have already experienced it. But what benefit will winning awards bring you and your business? You need to ask yourself – why do you want to win?

Winning business and personal awards can raise your profile, enhance your reputation and build trust – all vital ingredients for success in every walk of life. Award-winning companies attract new business and ultimately are more profitable. In summary, winning will independently prove you are better than your competitors.

So why should you enter awards?

As a business or an individual, they enable you to gain competitive advantage, achieve independent validation, generate free PR, boost team morale and secure trust in your business.

There are awards for everyone: from international to national, through to regional and local. These can be by sector and expertise, or by job role and demographic – there are literally hundreds of different awards available.

Obviously, there are pros and cons to the award entry process like there are to everything in business, but entering can become an efficient business development and promotion tool when you understand what is required. Let us share our experience from winning awards to make the journey easier for you and your business.

This book is split into sections that will take you through the whole award entry journey, covering where to find awards, how you can find the right ones for your business and what data you need to consider including. We will discuss the planning and research stages for your award entry, including the '5 Ws of winning'. This will then lead to the top tips for standout success, built around what the judges will want to see. We then discuss how to maximise your win to gain the greatest business benefit. Our ultimate aim is to develop a repeatable winning process for your business.

Having multiple insights is key to winning success – we have included wisdom from some major award winners, those who have been judges, and have run successful award programmes, as well as specialist knowledge from both a business psychologist and a PR-focused journalist to determine which factors will allow you to leverage the ongoing advantage awards can deliver for your business. Their combined awareness will help you to take your place on the winner's rostrum.

Has My Company Got What It Takes To Win An Award?

So, have you got what it takes to win an award? Almost certainly *yes*, unless you are particularly rubbish, and if you were particularly rubbish you probably would not be reading up on how to win awards, would you?

Every company will be different – you have got to determine what your company USP is – this is the Unique Selling Point that makes you stand out and makes your business memorable. Your USP could be focused on the company, or you as an individual. In many cases it is a combination of both.

Award entry provides the opportunity to showcase what you know you do well, and what your clients already tell you that you do well. The process involves putting that relevant information in a document that can be judged on that one single occasion. For this reason, an award entry is a snapshot of a business at a single moment or period of time. This is a key point – much like bids and proposals, the entry is judged on what you put down on that piece of paper at that moment – so you need to make it impactful and present the best version of the business.

Your clients probably love you; they think you are brilliant and are happy to sing your praises. If not, they will not remain clients for long, as they will seek excellence elsewhere.

Award entries give you the opportunity to document your achievements, but if you haven't done yourself justice on that entry form, they can't give you the credit, even if they are already aware of your business. Evidence is key, and what they might already know about you cannot be considered unless it is presented.

What does it take to win that award for your brilliant company? Well, you do need to choose the right award to enter, and you do need to take the necessary time to do your entry justice. This involves a planning stage, a scripting stage and the essential final proofing stage.

If the award entry deadline is looming, and you have made the last-minute decision that you are going to enter, you will certainly be in a better position if you have already structured your process knowledge and have a library of information whereby you can pull together all the requested support data. If you are scripting the entry on a very tight deadline with brand-new content, you need to recognise that your chances of success might be more limited. To give yourself the best chance, you will need to make that entry as part of a timely process, so you are not putting yourself under the pressure of a deadline. However, as Sheryl Sandberg is quoted: "Done is better than perfect." If you have a go and write from your heart, you are sure to learn and likely to succeed.

You also need to define what you class as a win. A new sparkly trophy is undoubtedly a win, a nice embossed certificate – that's a win. However, the win for you might actually be to attend a 'meet the judges' event to make a connection with the people that you would not have met otherwise. Or it could be the chance to develop a new client relationship. So, think about what your win actually is – the trophy might not be the sole reason for your entry, but undoubtedly it will be a motivation.

The focus of your effort needs to be in the creation of a compelling entry matched to the entry criteria. There are hundreds of awards to choose from and some awards are more heavily contested than others. National awards will undoubtedly have more competition than regional ones, which in turn will have more competition than local awards. You need to assess this and make the choice of which ones are best for you.

Debbie Gilbert, founder of the Best Business Women Awards and a multi-award winner herself, provides the following guidance: "If you have been in business for more than two years, ask yourself: Do you have satisfied customers, processes, and are you making a profit? Do you have a growth plan? If you can say *yes* then you should definitely consider entering awards. If you have been in business less than two years, consider a New Business category."

Isn't It Just the Big Companies That Win Awards?

No, but this is a common assumption. Of course big companies have more resources and there are certain awards that might favour big brands, because their agenda for running the awards might be to encourage a large company win. That way the award organisers can get the entrants to buy advertising space or sponsor an award in the future, or even buy a table of seats at the ceremony. However, there are many wonderful local, regional, national and sector focused awards that love to recognise great companies regardless of their scale, with no strings attached apart from the fact that they want you to have a great time.

This is where you do need to check the entry criteria – do they have a minimum turnover requirement? If so, they may be targeting larger companies. Also, research the previous winners – who took home the trophy in previous years? Is there a trend toward larger organisations with a national profile or toward companies of all sizes? Prior winners provide a good indication, but of course this is a reflection of the past – the awards may have changed focus and therefore the targeting may be different on this occasion. You do need to read the rules.

To give yourself the best chance, the entry criteria needs to be evaluated and matched against your individual and company attributes. This should be part of a business process, and each stage looked at impartially and without sentiment. Review how the awards are structured and calculate what can you gain out of them. You will only win if you can cross that finish line. "To finish first, first you must finish." And, if you don't put an entry in, you are not going to win, it is that simple.

Many people may say, "I could have won that" but did they actually bother to enter? Hats off to you if you have had a go, and congratulations if you are considering making an entry. You will increase your chances of winning by a huge magnitude because you have essentially filled out the form and had a repeatable, planned process. Awards entry will always provide the opportunity to learn and gain feedback, and you can be a winner regardless of the company size or area of expertise.

Visualise – Why Do You Want to Win?

Visualise that win. Understand why you want to win. When you know this, it will educate you as to the process you have to follow and the awards you will want to target to enter.

You might have numerous reasons for wanting to win – is it that gleaming trophy? Look at all those people at the Oscars or the

BAFTAs, waltzing down the winner's carpet clutching their adored icon. Do you want to be featured in the paper? Is having your photo and company name in print and online a big driver for you and your business? Do you want an invitation to the Palace or No 10, meeting with royalty and the powerful? Is that a lifetime achievement that you want to fulfil?

It might be that you are looking to raise your personal or your business profile. This could include gaining the respect and admiration of your industry. You may also want to stand out in your specific sector of expertise, so your business is recognised as a 'great' in that field. But also, don't rule out the importance of building trust. Award entries that are really strong usually have a large number of endorsements from those clients who value what is delivered. The whole process of winning awards is like an endorsement that helps those outside your network view your business as a safe pair of hands and a low-risk choice.

If someone outside the business has realised you are good and has been prepared to go on the record to say so, it is far more powerful than if you, as a business, say how good you are.

Winning awards and the recognition as an award-winning company is also important for recruiting new talent. People love to be part of a winning business. That might be the very first thing that they learn about you and seeing the award-winning badge can generate interest. So they have read about you and want to know more about what you do. This manifests a whole cycle of great PR: you have a raised profile, the business has a great reputation, you attract great talent, you win more awards, you win more clients, and your positive PR increases again. This can become a perpetual cycle.

You also may want recognition from your peers, so you are investigating the potential of targeting industry awards or those of specific membership associations. This can allow you to have that standout within your industry group and can help raise your profile as a thought leader within the industry to leverage speaker engagements or consultancy. This win might also be a route to developing peer partnerships that could lead to you working together on shared projects.

Winning new customers should be a major reason why you want to enter awards, because you then have the ceremonies, with the chance of networking, and the pre- and post-award social media activity that you can link in with. It is valuable to be able to say, "we have done this" and it can open your message up to a new audience, meaning you are able to secure new clients. Awards present the opportunity to reinforce relationships with your established clientele as well. You might have the chance to take your clients to the award ceremony with you, so the networking opportunity is magnified as they can then share in your success and feel a part of your business.

Winning a prize might also deliver a commercial benefit. You could choose to increase your prices, raising the perceived value in your marketplace of the product or service that you deliver. Award entry can also be driven by wanting to prove someone else wrong, or even as a reassurance to yourself. Is there a nagging voice in your head or from a member of your social circle? Did someone in the past say no, it is not a good idea, we don't think you have got what it takes, and you will never succeed at that? Sometimes the agenda for winning an award is that independent validation. To be able to say, "yes, I did achieve that" then the award is all about fulfilling that potential. A note of caution though, if your only driver is one-upmanship, you might find the victory hollow. Make sure you enter for your own reasons that give you power to move forward.

Visualise – Why Do You Want to Win?

- A gleaming trophy for your office?

- Being featured in the paper?

- An invitation to the Palace, or No 10?

- Raising your profile?

- Gaining the respect and admiration of your industry?

- Building trust in your business?

- Recruiting new talent?

- Recognition from your peers?

- Winning new customers?

- Attracting new opportunities?

- Facilitating a price increase for your services?

- Proving others wrong?

- Fulfilling your potential?

There Is an Award for You

So what sort of business are you? You might be a micro business, a solopreneur single-person organisation or happily self-employed. Or are you part of a larger corporation or a medium-sized business that has departments and structure? You could be an outstanding entrepreneur or do fabulous work within a charity or a social enterprise – whatever size of organisation – there is an award for you. Public sector bodies also have awards that you can enter.

There are awards that focus on businesses with specific structures, such as franchises, as well as market specialisms. If you are outstanding in your sector of expertise, there is no doubt there is an award out there with your name potentially on it.

With so many awards to choose from, you will need to go through a process of filtering, looking at the attributes of the entry requirements and understanding the accreditations they want from you. You will need to show the proof of your ambition. That's just the spark the judges are looking for: that you are prepared to learn, you are equipped to put yourself through the process and you are set to showcase your excellence.

Why Should You Enter Awards?

As you are reading this book, you likely already know how important entering and winning awards can be for the reputation and success of your business. But it is surprising how few awards companies enter; many don't realise what winning an award can do for them or don't want to spend the time and effort it takes to write a good entry. While this might be detrimental to their businesses, it is advantageous for anybody who does enter awards, as with a well-written and well-thought-out entry, lower entry numbers can increase your chances of success.

We have already summarised the benefits, but we will now consider these in more depth. You will need to appreciate the gain from your effort before you consider expending it – understand why you will use all this exertion and energy. So why should you enter? For most individuals and businesses, it's about gaining competitive advantage, and it is a way of leveraging previous goodwill to gain more clients in the future. Entering, being a finalist, and ultimately winning an award are great ways to showcase how good you are in your sector and achieve that highly desired independent validation.

But what exactly can winning, or being shortlisted for an award do for you, providing you make the most of the opportunity? Winning business and personal awards is all about raising profile, enhancing reputation, and very importantly, building trust – all vital ingredients for continued success in a competitive environment. Award-winning companies attract new business as they gain independent validation, which can mean they are ultimately more profitable. In a crowded marketplace with lots of noise, an award accolade will impartially prove you are better than your competitors. This is really significant, as an autonomous body or association has recognised – that in a given sector, geography, gender or structural location, at a specific timeframe, and under stated rules and classifications of the judges – that this entry was acknowledged as the winner.

Awards encourage people to view your business as an industry leader and thus, give you an edge over your competition. If you are a food brand, you may be viewed as having superior quality or taste, or a technology company may be viewed as having the most innovative and cutting-edge technology in their industry. Think about it – if you are in a shop, trying to choose between two almost identical products from two different brands, but one has won awards and the other hasn't, which are you likely to choose?

Enter awards and you will gain a competitive advantage

An award massively boosts both your business and your products' credibility in the eyes of consumers. This is because consumers no longer have to take your word for it that you're the best – outside, unbiased parties also agree. This provides a concrete seal of approval which evidences the quality of the products or the services you offer. Social proof is one of the most influential factors in a consumer's decision-making process, as many people are influenced by online customer service reviews. Awards in many ways are the ultimate testimonial – they come from an independent authority with the expertise to provide an informed judgment on your business, its products and its services – providing solid proof that you can be trusted.

Enter awards and you will achieve independent validation

Generating PR is a key element. Yes, awards are fabulous for generating PR coverage and provide many platforms at all stages of the entry process, but if you are feeling brave, you could state on your media channels that you entered, long before you find out whether you are actually a finalist. Many of you will not want to be that bold, but there are subtle ways you can do this, such as being invited and photographed at a launch event or sharing the request to enter on your social channels, so your business is helping with the promotion. Of course, the more entrants an award has, the more sponsorship it can gain and the bigger the awards can become in the future – all good news for the organisers.

Once you become a finalist, this is the traditional opening stage for a news story, so get a press release generated, upload it to your website and social media channels, as well as providing information to the media. Don't forget the traditional print channels as well as the online and business press. Share your message to say how delighted you are to be a finalist and how excited you are for the upcoming award ceremony to find out the results. Also take a moment to thank the organisers and to wish all the other finalists well.

When you have won is when you get the big guns blazing. This is usually the stage of most opportunity as people love to read about the success of others. The ways to maximise being a winner are covered later in the book, alongside advice from PR expert Fiona Scott who shares her thoughts as to what a journalist will want to see.

Obviously, you have to put in time, effort and resources to enter an award. However, particularly if the award is free to enter, exploiting the win as much as you can, can offer the biggest return on investment that you could get on any marketing strategy. A press release about your award win can be written and consequently picked up by relevant news publications. You can post and share about not only your win, but the award event itself on social media. The award ceremony provides excellent networking opportunities. All of these will increase your business's reach, visibility and potential opportunities.

Enter awards and you will generate valuable PR

One of the sometimes overlooked yet increasingly important aspects of winning awards is that awards are great for team morale. Many people recognise how tough being in business is. If you are an owner-managed business, it can be even harsher because you haven't got staff to share the journey with. If you are a small team, you are always under pressure, and if you are a large team, you can sometimes feel disconnected from each other. No matter the size of the business, having that reward of boosting morale enables people to talk positively about the business. It secures trust in your business because you have got that independent validation shared from within. When your staff are saying how great the business is, others will understand the importance and want to join the organisation. Emotional connectivity is a very credible way to recruit new talent.

An award provides official recognition to employees of their hard work and contribution, so they feel valued. It also affords validation to them that they can be proud of the company they work for. Ultimately, this can increase staff motivation and productivity and their positive attitude will reflect in both their work and attitude toward clients. The positivity created by working for an award-winning company cannot be underestimated.

Enter awards and you will provide a boost to your team morale

To get beyond the dreaming stage, you will need to face the reality of what you can present about your business. **Debbie Gilbert**, founder of the Best Business Women Awards, offers the following advice: "You need to understand whether this is the right time for your business to enter. Do you have a track record of achievement to present, and does your business have a story, if so how good?

"When you complete an award entry, it gives you the chance to look at your business from every angle, and this is an extremely useful exercise. You should review the competition and benchmark yourself against the market."

Debbie continues: "If you get shortlisted or win, you gain many benefits including credibility – an award gives you the edge against your competition and validates your work. PR opportunities – which will help to build your reputation, new business opportunities, and the chance to gain new clients, as well as providing something to shout about to existing clients. Don't forget the networking opportunities as well."

The entry process itself is a valuable one and the information gained during the preparation of the entry can be used to further refine your business operating procedures, so it is a hugely constructive and educational exercise. The benefits of being independently assessed and judged can be hugely important as this provides a badge of credibility that your business will possess well into the future.

An award win also acts as an aid to the buying decision – it is an indicator of business quality and stand out among the competition. Not only does it help new clients in their purchasing decision, it reaffirms the choice made by existing clients, helping with your business client retention.

Entering awards helps you to refine your own business story

And you do it to get this feeling!

Activity

- Make a list of the awards you have entered in the past – why did you choose them?

- What did you achieve as the result?

- Where do you currently look for awards to enter?

- What award types do you wish to target in the next two years?

Notes:

Business Psychology Related to Award Entry
by Jan de Jonge

Jan de Jonge is a business psychologist who helps organisations to improve the performance of their people and their business. He founded People Business Psychology Ltd. in 2012, to focus on the application of business psychology expertise in organisations. We asked Jan what some of the psychological principles behind award entry are and how they can help your business.

What actually is the winning feeling on a psychological level?

Winning awards is all about being entrepreneurial, being focused on building successes, gaining recognition for that success from one's peers and, more widely, the outside world – customers and potential customers included.

Science has identified several different neurotransmitters and hormones, some of which can actually be a neurotransmitter and a hormone at the same time, and some of which can be a hormone but not a neurotransmitter and vice versa. Dopamine, endocannabinoids, endorphins, adrenaline, and serotonin, many of these are often referred to as 'happy hormones', can work quite addictively. It's a very basic human biological process that goes on. We want something like affirmation of our own self-image and also of the image – hopefully a positive one – that we think others have of us.

Is there a dangerous side to experiencing a sense of euphoria when we win?

We have a perception of how others see us or praise us. It can also mean at a biological level that our brain process can almost become numb or blunted to that process of pleasure, so next time you need a bit more of it. That can be the addiction spiral.

The 'happiness hangover' can be an issue; the win might provide this intense pleasure or euphoria, but then you need to come back to a sense of what your natural emotional position is – your homeostasis. Much like skydiving where you would have the 'pain' or stress of falling and the sudden 180-degree reversal of it – the pleasure of having landed safely on earth.

In order to be able to channel that process over time, of dealing with reward success or the pleasure of it, or the acknowledgment, all these things, you also have to be able to cope with or deal with the rejection. It can be quite a demotivating thing that can happen to a person. Rejection can very quietly but ferociously eat away at our sense of self-esteem, of self-respect.

There are people who are less able than others to control themselves and have less mental strength. They might revert to outside sources or things around them to either hang on to that euphoria longer – hence the dangers of drugs, or smoking or excessive drinking, or even being amongst a 'clique' of similar people. They might seek people in similar situations as they are stuck in, who seem to adore them or make them feel wanted or accepted. Even excessive buying of goods: shopping addiction, buying 'stuff' – there are people that can't cope with it (or can't afford it) and look to fill the gap with other euphoric experiences instead.

There is also the idea of false expectations; there may be people who think that if they win X, Y, Z, that will be the kickstart for more success down the road. It may well be that some success acts as a motivator, but you need to keep that momentum going and that can be hard or perhaps even unrealistic. It's like these rock bands who have a successful debut album, and then they realise not only how hard it had been to create that first album, but also to replicate it for their next album.

So, one aspect is the idea that we might get used to the thrill of winning. Another aspect is that unconsciously we may expect to win again, the expectation of which influences subsequent behaviour. You could unknowingly cut yourself some slack, because clearly you know how it's done, but when doing it again, you realise that there was actually quite a lot of hard work involved – and you had forgotten and underestimated that. The sense of familiarity led to a false perception after the win that it had been easy, but reality proved different.

Another aspect is that you become used to the shine of the win the first time, like the feeling of having your first baby perhaps, the novelty of it. The experience then raises your level of what you feel is good. So, in order to get the same 'kick' out of it, you might need a slightly larger venue and a few more people in the audience to be present at the awards ceremony. You look for a higher investment level represented. It's a natural thing to set your goals higher and there's nothing wrong with that, as it is development and progress and human nature. The question is what's the meaning of it? What are we trying to achieve?

What is important is that for every award final, or every win, it is meaningful, it's worthy of being grateful for, and you are appreciating it. But with human nature there is a reality even after you have won; the dog still needs to be let out, there's shopping to be done... normal day-to-day life still goes on.

Can anyone win or is success determined by our personality type?

What does it take to be successful? Key variables that determine how successful a business (or, in a wider sense, an organisation) and the people in that business may be are personal ability, levels of motivation, personality and the context.

In assessment as part of business psychology or occupational psychology, we aim to predict behaviour. We look at the question of someone's ability, and we decide on ways in which to measure and test these candidates. For example, to find out if someone's going to be successful in learning how to fly an aeroplane, we conduct various tests to discover their ability to absorb a myriad of incoming signals and information and translate it into narrowly defined activities to control a multi-million pound flying machine with passengers and crew inside it.

Apart from that, we also want to know 'to what extent is that person able to remain calm when something happens up in the sky' using the same example of flying. What it boils down to in this context is calmness and it's about personality. Not only abilities of your personality but also your tendencies of how you behave and your preferences even. Do you prefer to be dominant or follow the lead of someone else? Would you be a great co-pilot, or do you want to sit in seat number one?

The other thing that is important is the question of whether you want it. You can be a fantastic fighter pilot and you can have the right characteristics in terms of personality to be able to be happy and fulfilled in that kind of work, but do you want to do it? So, motivation is a third dimension. The fourth dimension is the context.

The answer is no, not everyone can do it. You have to have certain ingredients, and certain levels of them. So while winning awards may not be determined by a personality type, it's highly influenced by a person's make up, a person's personality.

I would like to explore the third aspect of personality a little more. People who are more likely to be successful in business, whether that be beginning a new startup micro business or helping to develop and grow an existing business, tend to possess the following characteristics: *creativity* – people are more entrepreneurial when they are imaginative and enjoy creating new ideas. Such people are more inclined to do away with old-fashioned ways of doing things and embrace innovation, even if this goes against accepted norms. They will be more inclined to produce a range of alternatives that have not been tested yet, and they show flexibility in their thinking and their approach.

Another aspect to creativity is the ability of people to be alert to a need for change or innovation. That is, some people may not be creative or resourceful themselves, but they are discerning and alert to opportunities that present themselves in some way and are able to let others around them creatively respond to that gap in the market, that they themselves were able to spot.

Assertiveness – people who are entrepreneurial need to have a certain level of confidence in themselves and a sense of independence. They are relatively self-directed and determined, and they believe in their ideas or suggestions. At the same time, they are willing to test these against realism. The latter is helped by the intersocial aspect of their personality: entrepreneurial people are able and willing to seek out and nurture interpersonal relationships. Where they are less eager to do so, they understand that they may need to learn the relative skills. A simple way of putting this is that more successful entrepreneurs are more likely to enjoy networking, for instance.

Resilience – people who are entrepreneurial are those who have tried and tried again, or tried something different (and again). They are more able than others to cope with pressure and setbacks. And before that, they are less inclined to let a fear of failure obstruct them from putting their ideas to the test. They pick themselves up when things go against them and brush off criticism more easily – they may take it less personally than some. One of the key components of what some refer to as 'emotional intelligence' is the ability to regulate one's emotions and tolerate stress. This influences how a person is able to anticipate and deal with the challenges of building a business as an entrepreneur.

Enterprising people are those who not only 'can do', but those who actually 'do'.

A 'do-attitude' is different to a 'can-do' attitude. Many people might well say they possess entrepreneurial intent or are enterprising but there is a difference between those who not only can-do but actually 'do'. These individuals are able to convert their confidence into real and measurable action. This means that they are more proactive, more purposeful and productive and may have higher levels of energy (that they put to use), tenacity and drive. Towards the opposite of the do-attitude is the can-do attitude, where people may ponder and plan and prepare but not progress to the phase of 'production', of 'doing'.

Optimistic insightfulness – people are more likely to be successful as entrepreneurs when they have an optimistic attitude, an optimistic default position, that they are able to combine with a healthy dose of commercial acumen and ability to understand complexities.

The above personality characteristics can be measured. A great deal of research suggests that these measurements, when done properly (i.e. using valid and reliable techniques), can help to predict the success of people in business. Creativity, assertiveness, resilience, a do-attitude, and optimistic insightfulness are five ingredients that are relevant for success in winning in business.

However, there are many examples where businesses have been created or have become hugely successful despite one or more of these ingredients being in shorter supply. Besides this, the notion of complementarity suggests that, with enough insight into the make up of individuals, the members of a team can help each other to achieve success as a team.

Is attitude toward risk a factor in award-winning success?

There are tools that measure people's so-called 'risk type' or the way that an individual manages the way that he or she may welcome or deal with risk. If you're like most others, then you can sometimes be excitable, and you can be deliberate. If you are more easy-going with risk than a lot of people, then you are considered to be carefree or even adventurous, or bold. Those that are on the opposite end of the scale are wary.

Another way of answering it is by looking at personality again, your risk aversion. The extent to which that is the case for someone is very much a personality trait. The received wisdom in psychology nowadays is that personality is thought of as consisting of five big factors. The extent to which you deliberate your actions is no doubt related to the extent to which you are successful in dealing with risk, because if you don't deliberate enough, you are more inclined to do foolish things.

Another important factor is openness – the openness to ideas and a wide range of input from the world around you. If someone is more open to ideas than others, then they will embrace the idea of running for a certain bid or an award more easily than someone who says 'that's not part of me, that's not what we do'.

What are the feelings associated with finding out we did not win? How do we overcome these and move on?

It follows the model of how you deal with grief and the stages of that. Initially, you might have a sense of disappointment, you might even be angry that others were more successful than the person who has lost. Self-doubt might even come into it as well by feeling sorry for yourself and thinking that you never have any luck. So, the whole process of putting the blame on someone other than yourself.

The fundamental attribution error comes into play here, which says that people tend to, in the wrong way, emphasise external factors as the cause of someone's behaviour or someone's level of success. This may happen when we don't want to acknowledge to ourselves that we are not skilled enough, or that we could have done better, or that we didn't put enough energy into it.

Feedback and self-awareness are key terms in all of this. Being self-aware and self-critical, and being open to feedback from other people who might confirm that 'yes, this is where you went wrong' or 'that's where you could have done better', can be hard to swallow. The notion of pride comes into play there as well.

According to that fundamental attribution error, people will explain their loss, or their lack of a success, to the outside world.

But, their successes they may attribute to their own personality or their own actions.

Will the psychological process of entry actually improve my attitude about my business?

I think it's the alternative way of doing some self-coaching, because if you do it well, it takes time and investment. It forces you to hold up a mirror of self-analysis. The psychological process is opening up to self-reflection, to self-analysis, and measuring where you were, and where you are, and where you want to be. That then shapes not necessarily the attitude to the business, but certainly makes clearer what you were up to, and whether it was right or wrong, or whether that approach should be adapted.

It also comes down to what kind of mindset you have and what your expectations were, how self-determined you are, how much self-discipline you've had and whether you should up the ante on the self-discipline. What do you allow yourself, what do you say to yourself, what do the team say to themselves, in terms of how we go about our business? Have we got our goals clearly defined, are they realistic enough, is the cashflow healthy enough in order to keep business activities going for a certain amount of time?

Aspects that relate to one's attitude are, for instance, the extent to which we are able to, or want to, open up about how successful or not we actually are or have been. Is it as successful as we made it out to be? Or are we strong enough to show that we are not actually as successful as we would love to be able to say?

The fear of failure comes into play and understanding that, just by being in the frame and putting yourself up for an award, it at least puts you in the picture of that target audience and whether or not you win… is a different matter altogether. The fact that you show your ambition should be part of that positive attitude of wanting to win. It's not all about winning at all; it's wanting to win that's more important.

The extent to which someone can be competitive is a basic, natural personality trait in most people whatever their culture is, as it's a cross-cultural level of competitiveness. Another way of looking at it is that some people live in the here and now and enjoy their days, whereas some just live for tomorrow and they forget about today. It's all about achieving tomorrow and debuting in their next step of success rather than them being mindful of what they have already.

What effect does confidence play in the chances of winning?

One way of looking at it is asking where that word comes from. 'To confide', the Latin behind it is from the verb 'to trust', and 'con' means placing your trust in someone. To have confidence you need to have confidence in yourself. Trusting that you can do it, you are worthy of it.

A derivative of going for an award is the idea that underneath it… is a message of aspiration. The fact that you get yourself out there and want to be acknowledged also says something about where you see your vision; you have to have some aspiration. It's not the end of the end, the award is a step in. It's more about long-term achievement and fulfilment. It's like a strategic message, it says 'I have ambitions'. It's not just that hunger for short-term acknowledgment you're aiming for. Ideally, all your shorter-term activities are aligned with the longer-term goals that you feel you are able to achieve, for the benefit of as many people around you as possible.

Thanks so much for that wonderful insight Jan!

What Are the Best Awards to Enter?

As you will now appreciate, there are many different types of awards and finding the best ones to enter to optimise your chance of success is somewhat of a challenge – you will need all your effort to be rewarded.

Finding the right awards to enter is just as important as a well-written award entry. Not looking in the right places and entering awards that don't match your business will be a significant waste of your time and resources, as you will be unlikely to get through the process. Not only that, you will become demoralised.

As the entry process is going to demand resources of both time and effort, you don't want to be entering the ones that you haven't got a chance of winning. It is, however, important to recognise what the win is for you and your business. While the title and trophy may be the ultimate goal, it could be that the win will help to build a relationship or provide the opportunity to visit a prestigious venue that you would never have the occasion to attend otherwise. For most people and companies, you need to know which awards will provide the most focused platform to showcase your skills and deliver the opportunity to shine. You need to assess the structure of the awards and how they can feature your USPs to your greatest advantage to make you stand out.

You don't have to be the best in the world or in the UK or even the best in your sector – you must be the best out of the people who entered. This can't be emphasised enough; the entry is not about competing against the universe – merely the other entrants.

Many organisations worry about comparing themselves to much more established businesses, or those with larger turnover or higher profile successful clients. Despite this, it is important to be the one who actually enters, as most businesses can win awards if they go about it the right way.

Are you back to visualising why you want to win? Doesn't winning seem lovely? You must analyse what kind of recognition it will deliver for your business, because that is the motivation for you. Is it a personal vision? What do you want? What effort are you prepared to put in to get it?

The good news is that you are not short on choices in the broad spectrum of awards you can target. There are international awards with global recognition, but they are going to be a lot harder to win as there will be a greater target audience of potential entrants. If you have what it takes – go for it – the reward for being an international winner is going to be huge and the ultimate in prestige.

National awards are also major accolades – the kudos of having a national title is massive, but that's not to say that as a small business you can't leverage great PR out of winning a local award. You must have a strategy – which awards are going to deliver the best leverage for what you are trying to achieve?

If you are looking to attract clients within a given sector, then go for a sector-based award.

Purpol Marketing are delighted to have won the Construction Enquirer Top Ten Supplier Award for two consecutive years. It was matched to our sector specialism of bid writing and marketing within the construction sector and we made a specific choice of which target audience we wanted to promote ourselves into. The awards presented a great networking opportunity, national PR coverage within the sector and a chance to raise our profile, which in turn led to more speaking engagements – that's a lot of wins out of one award entry process! Added to this was the chance of a live TV interview within a major building expo, which was, as expected, highly beneficial.

We were beamed around the National Exhibition Centre in Birmingham.

We assessed the entry criteria – the grouping for the businesses that we entered against was turnover up to £25 million. We are nowhere near that, but as we have identified, you have got to look at what is going to be the effort relative to the opportunity leverage you might gain.

By being a finalist in industry specific awards, you may gain publicity through a channel that is specific for your target audience. There are awards in every sector imaginable – from recruitment to financial services, from leadership and coaching to HR. There is every classification of every award you could think of.

You can also enter awards focused on specific job roles: e.g. an architect, a teacher, or a florist. If you are in that given role and you want the platform to stand out against your peers, then you are sure to find it. There are also awards by gender and even by age classification – every demographic is covered and waiting to provide you with the opportunity to be a winner.

You have got to decide which ones you think will provide the best return for your effort.

The list of available awards is constantly updated, so we recommend that you subscribe to one of the major award monitoring websites. They will send you a list of awards every month that you can select from. These include www.boost-awards.co.uk and www.boostawards.com.

How to Find the Right Awards for Your Business

As we have already discussed, there is a vast spectrum of awards that cover numerous subjects. So while recognising the different choices available, you will need to assess by a robust and impartial method, which ones best fit you and your business at the current time. Even within a single award type, there may be different categories that you can enter.

It is worth having an open mind on what you could be eligible for. Within regional and local awards you may have a chance to recognise a regional office, and if you have offices in different locations, it could be worth applying in several different regions for different sets of expertise or personnel to be recognised. Have a look to see if there are awards related to your town or county. Your Local Enterprise Partnership or Growth Hub may have a recognition platform. Don't forget the membership associations and chambers of commerce that you are part of as well.

If you have a wealth of awards to choose from, have a look at the previous winners. Do you want to be associated in the space that they are in? This can be a really good way of filtering which awards you want to look at and can educate your effective choice of category. You need to consider which one will give you the greatest credibility as a winner. It is also worth considering having a primary first choice category and a secondary one.

Having been through the entry process and assessed all the criteria, to write the second award entry might not be a huge amount of additional effort, having completed the initial one. Look at what is needed – can you just tweak it here and there? You could potentially double your chances of success!

Look at the awards title. Would you be proud of winning? While you are unlikely to bother entering something you don't want to win, there might be awards among the list that don't immediately jump out at you. When you are going through that filtering process, don't dismiss the more obscure categories which often have fewer entrants.

> Don't miss out on winning because you overlooked a category. We decided to enter the NatWest GB Entrepreneur of the Year Awards and focused our initial efforts on the 'Service Business' category award, but after a review, also decided to have a go at the 'Go-Do Entrepreneur of the Year' category.

Tailoring our entry to my entrepreneurial journey, I was amazed and delighted to win the Go-Do Entrepreneur of the Year title and was even serenaded on stage by Mr 'GoCompare', Wynne Evans. More on that story later…

Check, can you answer all the questions? This might sound obvious, but if there are responses that you are not confident in, this will affect the overall likelihood of success. If you are asked to submit a business plan – do you want to reveal your future direction? If you are asked for accounts – do you want to reveal this level of financial detail?

If you have an issue, there is always a route – ask the question. If in the entry criteria they say they want three years' worth of accounts, and you are a startup and there's no startup award, you can actually ask a clarification question of the judges and state your situation so you can understand if entry is worthwhile. If you think you match the criteria on other grounds, you need to review if it is worth going through the process. Most people will enter into a dialogue with you to help you out. You need to impartially assess whether this specific award is a good return on your effort, or whether you will be better placed to wait a year to go after the award next time.

This will sometimes need to be a corporate decision taken by a board, but if you are an individual in a business, talk to one of your trusted peers and get their opinion. There are variations in risk attitude, so review what is required against what you might gain from the process. You must be quite hard on yourself to assess how well you will stand up against other entrants. Are you good enough to take the title matched to the presented judging criteria? If yes, then place yourself against your peer group regionally, nationally or internationally.

Many of you will underestimate your own or your company's brilliance so get a reliable second opinion. If you have got what it takes, then you should definitely go for it, but have an open mind and remember that it is all a learning experience. In the cold light of day, consider which award entries are most relevant for your business and make sure they are worthy of your efforts.

Find the Right Awards to Enter

- Look at previous winners – do you want to be associated with them?

- Choose the right category – which one will give the greatest credibility?

- What is the award title – would you be proud of winning?

- Check – can you answer all the questions thoroughly?

- Assess – are you good enough to take the title?

- At least one YES – and you definitely should enter!

As part of the award category assessment process, you need to identify whether there is a specific category that you want to stand out in. Do you really want to be known as an entrepreneur, a coach or a leader? What about the best of your industry specialism? If you have limited resources then target the one you really want, find out the structure and then the entry can be tweaked for any additional submissions. If you are going through the process, then what have you got to lose? Success in one classification is not dependent on another one, and it is perfectly possible to come home with more than one trophy from a single awards ceremony.

> So, can you really have more than one win at a ceremony? YES – we did it. Purpol had this magnificent outcome at the Women of the Year Awards in 2017. We managed to take home three awards in one evening. This really proved that the independent judging process of one category was not influenced by another. We got amazing PR, everyone saw us collect an award on multiple occasions, and even after three 'walks of fame' we did not fall up the stage steps. Taking home all these awards had another amazing benefit – they played Prince's Purple Rain in celebration of such a Purpol occasion. This was further brand reinforcement and an additional delight as a Prince fan!

The right award for you is one where you have a good chance of winning. Therefore, you need to review what will deliver this success. You need to consider some of the following points: When is the deadline? If it falls when everybody in your team is on holiday, is it going to be tricky to get the entry process completed? If you have a long entry period, it makes sense to get prepared in advance as time soon disappears and the opportunity may be lost. Work back from the deadline to understand what is achievable. On the positive side, if everyone in your industry is on holiday, then you may have a better chance, as others will also be under pressure with limited staffing levels.

Also, make sure to assess the obscure categories. Is there one that you think: "I've got no idea what they are looking for in this, but why don't we go for it?" If it's more obscure the chances are fewer people will enter. In regional awards for example, the small business category or the medium business, and the business leader are all high entry categories. The ones that reward environmental sustainability or training often have fewer entries because they ask very specific questions in the entry. So, it might be worth considering what your business can deliver against these factors, and if it is a subject you are passionate about, such as providing internships and apprenticeships, you will be able to prove you stand out. Make considering the less obvious choice part of your assessment process – the obscure one could be the one that you stand out in!

When trying to decide which award or category of an award to enter, you need to consider the relevance that the award can have to your business as there are no awards that encompass the entire business world. The awards you could possibly win, or want to win, will depend on your industry, what kind of authority you would like to build and your business network. For example, a food industry business would likely be more interested in gaining awards that compare them against other food providers rather than, say, an award for best community impact – which might be more important to a healthcare service or even a recruitment agency.

You will also want to explore the opportunities in your business network. Your suppliers or some of your strategic alliance partners may run awards, or know of awards, for which you may be a suitable applicant. Choose your category wisely. Some categories are always going to be more popular than others and so will get the most entries. If you think you can write a good submission for a slightly more obscure category, you will boost your chances of winning significantly.

The main factors in summary are:

- Can you supply the information the award requires?

- Is there one particular category you think you will stand out in?

- Do you think it is worth applying for more than one category?

- Can you meet the award deadline?

- Have you got enough time to write a quality entry?

Debbie Gilbert, founder of the Best Business Women Awards wisely comments: "Check industry awards and local awards. Read the categories avidly to check if you fit the criteria. Be very careful to read the application thoroughly and give the judges exactly what they are asking for."

Another factor to consider is the possibility of entry fees. Not every award will attach costs to the entry, but some will, and it is important for you to consider whether it is worth entering. If you think you have a significant chance of winning, you have the time and energy to devote to creating the perfect entry and the award itself is a well-recognised and respected award, then it may well be worth the money. However, if you cannot answer yes to these three considerations, then you should really judge whether the time and money spent on an award could be better spent elsewhere.

Regarding entry fees, it is important to remember that there are a lot of awards that are free to enter, with just the ceremony itself requiring payment. Free awards provide just as much potential leverage as paid awards with less risk attached, especially for smaller businesses.

However, some awards use a minimal entry fee as a filter to encourage quality entries and remove time wasters from the judging process. This can be important in focusing the entry process and making sure that a value is attributed to the effort being made.

Insight From Previous Award Winners

We invited experts from across different business areas to share what they have learned from the award entry process, and to explain what value they have gained from being award winners.

Caroline Sparks and Gaby Lixton from Turtle Tots are highly successful award winners, having successfully launched and established Turtle Tots as an innovative and unique swimming programme in 2011. Turtle Tots now has licensees across the UK and Ireland.

Roni Savage is the Founder and Managing Director at Jomas Associates, specialists in contaminated land and geotechnical engineering. Roni is a chartered engineering geologist and provides expertise in environmental and geo technical engineering within the construction industry. Roni is passionate about women in engineering and social mobility.

We asked Caroline, Gaby and Roni about the awards they have won, and if they had focused on particular awards to enter.

You have been really successful in winning business awards in the past, please tell us about the awards you have won.

Caroline and Gaby:

> Over the last eight years, we have won several awards. The first one for Mumpreneur of the Year in 2013 at the Startups Awards. That was the first award we had ever won, and it was really amazing to feel that we had been recognised. What we liked about these awards was that they were not just judged by the number of votes – we prefer to enter

awards where there is a credible panel of judges looking at your application.

Then we won the Regional Business Leader Award and are the only company that has won awards with them for three years running. We also won the Best Franchise which was run by the Best Business Women Awards, and were a regional winner in the Forward Ladies awards a couple of years ago as well.

We have been finalists in a number of other awards too, but what its really meant to us is that people have obviously heard about our business and think it's an award-winning business model. It recognises our achievement and it is also something that we can use for PR and gives us credibility when we are looking at attracting new licensees.

Roni agrees that entering awards has had a huge impact on her business.

Where do I start? Last year was a great year for me and it started off with being listed within the Top 100 Female Executive Role Models and also the Top 100 Ethnic Minority Executives by the *Financial Times* and EMpower, which was great, and then a number of others including the NatWest Athena Inspirational Woman Award; the Black British Business Person of the Year; the Precious Awards Entrepreneur of the Year, the Best Business Woman in STEM, and the Venus Awards Entrepreneur of the Year.

As a business we won the Construction Enquirer Best Consultant to Work For, and the Precious Awards SME of the Year. This year I was named Best Consultant and Most Distinguished winner at the European Women in Construction and Engineering Awards. These were amazingly proud moments that blew me away.

Have you focused on a particular type of award to enter?

Caroline:

Initially we entered everything and anything we could. Then we really looked at what awards we were entering and focused on the investment. Although a lot of the awards were free to enter, some awards involved a judging day in London, which alongside dinner, hotel costs and trains to London, made it quite expensive to become a finalist. This process taught us to assess the return on investment and the publicity so we can determine if entry is worthwhile.

We review the awards we are entering, as these are very much about our licensee business promotion. What we started to do over the last couple of years is enter awards that aren't as expensive if we do become finalists. We also target awards that promote the actual swimming programme, so they are more consumer-focused awards, and these are the ones that parents will recognise if they are looking at swimming classes for their child.

The most recent awards that we have entered and won are an international award, which is the Mom's Choice Award, and we have entered our swimming programme into the UK Active Awards, which is a kids' award to encourage, engage, promote and sustain physical activity. Although we still are entering some business focused awards, I think our approach has changed, where we now enter a limited number of those, and we enter more awards which actually recognise the swimming programme itself.

Roni:

To be fair, I didn't know much about all the awards for many years because I was focused on building my business. I enjoy being an engineer and that was very much my sole focus, and then I was nominated for a couple of awards. It is really humbling to be nominated by people who I have a lot of respect for, especially when they have nothing to gain from it personally.

What I am doing now is also passing on the favour to the amazing people I am surrounded by – nominating them for awards that they might not enter themselves. I wouldn't have even thought about putting myself forward for some of the awards I have been successful in, including the Precious Awards and the Black British Awards, where I just got an email to say that I had been nominated. To then win, was such an honour.

It's great to be nominated, and then often they want to know more about you, so you have to put the effort in to complete the questionnaires. They can be daunting, but are certainly worth it, whether you are simply a finalist, or you actually win.

Be Aware – Not All Awards Are Created Equal

Congratulations, you have now identified the awards that you want to target, but you need to know when you are entering awards, whether the promoter has a specific agenda. Someone, be it an individual, organisation or association, is running these awards – so WHY are they doing it?

The vast majority of awards are ethical, enjoyable experiences but, like all aspects of life and business, there are always a few bad eggs to watch out for. That is not to say that even the following types of awards are bad in all aspects – what you need to be aware of is the whole picture around the entry process so that you can make an educated decision as to whether you want to partake.

Revenue generation might be a key factor in running an awards programme. This could be in the form of a high entry fee, an obligation to buy a given number of award ceremony tickets, or even to buy support advertising or sponsorship alongside the event.

Many awards do have a cost to enter, and you can understand why. If they expect a large number of entries, a minimal charge acts to put off those who will not make the desired effort in their application. A fee tests the resolve of the applicant, so that those who do enter acknowledge that the judging process will be robust. We cover the judging process later, as well as gaining feedback from some expert judges on what they look for in entries. Many of these experts are highly esteemed business peers – they are rarely paid for their judging activity and do it because they want to give back and share knowledge. However, a judging session may take several days, so they need plenty of tea and coffee (cakes and biscuits are also essential!).

Consider the entry fees as part of the process. Will the benefits outweigh the cost? There are certain awards where there is a negligible entry fee, so it is definitely not the case that if there's an entry fee then don't enter. You need to look at the full cost to enter. Certain awards are run by charitable institutions or businesses who need that help to make the judging process financially viable. If it's an award that you feel very positively toward, and you want to support it, then please do so. A likely range of entry fee might be £30-£80 rather than £300-£400 or even thousands. So, if you want to be part of the awards, and you have made the choice with full knowledge of the potential positive impact it could have for your business, then the very best of luck.

Sometimes the prestigious awards very deliberately have a higher value entry fee, because they want to attract larger corporate client entries and also cut down on the number of applications they need to read. Lesser competition might be an advantage, but you will still need to match against the criteria and stand out against those others who have put themselves through the process.

You may also come across the variant of an award with an entry fee that includes a ticket to the final. If you plan on attending the ceremony anyway, that is not going to be an issue, and if you are a finalist then that is great, your seat is booked, and the organiser will want you to be there. But if you are not successful in reaching the finals this time, the ticket may have negligible value for you. It shows great positivity and may even be a worthwhile investment to attend even if you are not a finalist, but you do have to consider how you will be feeling – you might prefer to attend when you know there is a chance of winning.

You can usually identify the awards which are designed purely as income generators – they will have statements in the terms and conditions that you must accept. On being a finalist you agree to attend the award ceremony and the ticket price is £500 per person. It might well be a very nice dinner, could have fabulous entertainment and potentially delightful company, and if that is the case and you think you can benefit, then go for it. You make the choice based on a full understanding – but please make sure you assess the return on investment of both your time, effort and cash for what you gain out of that specific singular award process.

The cost to your business isn't just the BACS payment or the direct debit. It's the time, the effort, the focus, the resources and the lost opportunity cost (time you could spend doing something else). Make that educated and conscious assessment of the true cost to enter.

There is also the strange phenomenon of being a finalist in awards you are sure you did not enter. Now it might be that a member of your team or a friend recommended you, in which case this is a great compliment and the prize is likely well merited. However, we do want to make you aware of what we charitably call the 'alternative' award process, so you can be fully cognisant of the implications and potential ramifications for your business.

There you are, happily sitting at your desk, when an email pops up. We have now seen several iterations of this, but you will see the pattern:

Congratulations, Denise and the team at Purpol Marketing, you have been recognised as the winner of the Best Marketing Strategy Agency in the UK.

To receive your crystal award please send £1,500 plus VAT and shipping and we will send you your trophy.

But we knew that we did not enter, and it was not an award that we recognised – what was this all about?

So, what are you offered for the £1,500 package? You can be featured in a publication, have a double-page promotional advert or editorial, two personalised crystal trophies, a digital winners' logo and be included on their website.

Maybe you fancy the medium-priced offer of around £800 that might provide a single-page editorial and a single personalised crystal trophy? Or perhaps the half-page variant for £400. If you are feeling more extravagant, you might wish to get on the front cover for a few more thousand pounds… but only if you are quick.

As time goes on, you get more emails including the encouragement that time is running out, the price might go down a bit but 'it would be a real shame if you weren't to receive anything in recognition'. You are then asked to email your acceptance, and of course they are happy to help if you have any questions.

We have actually had quite a few variations of this email. From the Best Bid Writing Agency in the South West through to the Best Marketing Agency in the UK, as well as awards associated to individual named towns and cities. None of these were entered, nor nominated by our clients.

If you wish, it is also usually in the small print, you can request your certificate for free by email. You will note that all of these communications come out of the blue, from people you probably don't know and include a read receipt so they can see if the email has been opened.

Here you have two choices – if you want to pay for the award, then by all means do so, shout about it on social media, put it in pride of place in the cabinet. But BEWARE, others in your network may understand this 'promotional mechanism'. Do you want your clients thinking that you had to buy an award to be able to win it?

The choice is yours but please do your research. Our view is that those awards that are independently judged by ethical means are of far greater value to your business.

Caroline:

> I am always slightly wary of a brand-new award and would discuss with the event organisers to find out a bit more. Some awards are much more established, and you can see what the past winners achieved as a result of that award. Have a really good look at the website and each listing. Award entries can take a few hours to enter and it is something you have to really put your head down, close the door and do. It is your time as well as all the financial implications of attending dinners and judging days, so I would just be really clear about what you think the return on investment will be.
>
> I tend to avoid awards which are just based on the number of votes you get, as we want to go for awards that recognise the quality of our programme rather than just the number of customers we have got. Sometimes you come across ones that you haven't heard of so just look at the website to verify them first.

Finding Awards To Enter

This is a very fast-moving field, with entries closing every week, if not every day, so where do you find those awards to enter? Is there a secret to where you should look?

There are numerous ways you can increase your chances of finding out about awards that are published, and this is without paying someone to find them for you.

A Google search for 'business awards' or 'business awards for small businesses' or business awards in your county, city, town, etc, is a good place to begin looking for awards to enter. You should also search for industry specific awards – if you are a construction company, Googling construction awards will bring up results such as the 'Construction Enquirer Awards'.

The first point of call is the internet (of course). Set up Google Alerts so that you are notified when awards are promoted. You will need to identify the keywords associated with the type of awards you are looking for – so this might be your sector, your knowledge, your expertise and your geography. The train of words in your search could include a few words or more detail. Keep it broader and you will potentially find more awards, but you will have to search through more information as a result.

Identify these keywords as part of your award entry strategy and then adjust them based on the results they present. Examples could include: 'Accountancy Awards London', 'Entrepreneur Service Business Awards', 'Manufacturer Awards Midlands', 'Female Leader Awards', 'Young Charity Champion Awards', etc.

Also keep up-to-date with publications and newsletters from your relevant industry bodies. Keep a search open on Google for the specific sectors that you are involved with. Don't forget all other forms of marketing and promotional communication such as websites, newsletters, blogs and emails. There is lots of information out there and trade association websites provide plenty of great content that can help you focus your entry for the greatest impact.

Chambers of commerce, membership organisations and regional bodies such as Growth Hubs and Local Enterprise Partnerships are also useful sources of information. As well as networking events and chatting to your business colleagues, don't forget the publishing media houses – they are very often part of the award organisational structure and will be promoting their awards both on their websites and across their social media platforms. We recommend that you find out as much as you can, to gain as much knowledge as possible, so you can select the most appropriate ones to target.

Also consider your suppliers and business partners. Do you have any strategic alliances with specific organisations? Understand the depth of your network and leverage relationships to find out about the awards you could enter. Do you have a PR agency, or do you have a friend who works in PR that could look out for awards for you? Do you have a network of people you think are always winning awards? Where do they find them? Understand the knowledge within your network and tap into it to gain information.

Have you thought of looking at competitor websites? It sounds very bizarre that you look there, but if your competitors are winning multiple awards, the chances are they are publishing the sort of awards they have won. Look at their news pages and identify how you can leverage that knowledge. You may choose to enter those awards next time around, or you might even avoid them – but at least you will know.

Previous award recipients are likely to promote their winning history – see later in the book for our 'ROAR – What to Do When You Win' chapter. Past winners are likely to be making a lot of noise about their success, after all that was one of the reasons they wanted to win in the first place. In all likelihood, they are promoting the awards they have won on their website – remember to look for those 'winner medals' in the footers of their emails too.

Also, consider whether to sign up to the email list of specialist awards agencies. Yes, there are specialist award entry agencies. Their role is to help people and businesses win awards of many different sorts. They do of course charge a fee to write the entry, and depending on the complexity of the process, this can be quite a significant investment. Knowing these agencies provide this service, they need a pipeline of awards to promote.

Many of these agencies can send you a newsletter, a 'here's the upcoming awards you might be interested in' communication. These emails are worth subscribing to as they collate detailed databases on upcoming awards, often sorted by expertise and by closing date, which means you can target the most relevant ones. Be prepared for them to approach you as they will want to help you with your entry, but of course recognise that is the reason they spend the effort developing the lists. If you subscribe, you will benefit from another data source.

At the end of the day, any help in identifying the vast array of awards in the market at a point in time is useful. It is a huge job to stay on top of the collation process and keeping abreast of what awards are out there, as new ones are launched all the time. If you have a few different sources of information, you will be able to see the universe of choice available and then select the international, national or sector specific award that is best aligned to your business.

Remember, award opportunities don't tend to fall in your lap. You need to go out and find the right ones for your business.

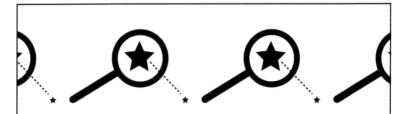

Finding Awards to Enter

Find out as much as you can — knowledge is power!

Where to look:

- Google

- Industry bodies

- Websites, newsletters, blogs, emails

- Chambers of commerce

- Trade association websites

- Media / publishing houses

Activity

- Make a list of the award types you think you would like to enter

- Which are the target awards from this list?

- Research the previous winners and commit to these

Develop a Process

Now you know which award you want to target and have assessed the benefits and chance of success; you might want to consider building yourself a target award plan.

Your award-winning strategy should be an element of your overall marketing plan and broader business plan. Within this blueprint, you need to assess which awards you want to target, and identify the benefits you believe this will bring for your business. It might be that 'a win is a win' and you would be happy to win any award. If you just want to win one because you can then say your business is an 'award winner', that is a perfectly respectable reason. It is more likely, however, that what you want to do is say, "I want to be a winner and I also want to be known for a given expertise within a specific sector". Examples of this might include "winner of best customer service in the healthcare sector", "best staff training in the recruitment sector", or "best hairdresser in the North West". So, look at all of those awards that exist, understand which ones you want for which reason, and build yourself that target list.

We can assure you that, from our experience, all your desirable awards will come along like buses! They will all arrive at the same time and will have similar submission dates. That is the way of the world (and may be the result of those who set up awards in competition to already successful ones). There is definitely an awards season in the business award arena, which seems to peak with entries open at certain points during the year, with the ceremonies themselves scheduled during the quieter period.

Recognising the seasonality of awards allows you to plan activity during the year. Once you have an awards plan and an entry process, you can build a winning momentum. Following a good result, where you know the detail you have written has been successful, you can use this information and update subsequent entries.

It is also prudent to review your success by entry category. It might be that in certain categories you have always got to the final, you know if you put together a good submission, and play by the rules, then generally you can get through. Your entry can only be judged against those who submit on that occasion, and on another attempt your ability to stand out may have improved, your business has grown, or you have delivered a new USP that has wowed the judges. You may also hit a year where there are fewer entrants – this does not devalue your success, as you still took the effort to submit when many of your peers did not.

Once you have analysed your results, you can then look to get feedback which will be hugely valuable and informative in directing your entry next time. Building in these improvements will increase your chances of success in the future.

There might also be awards where you want to 'maintain your crown'. This is true for many agencies, such as recruitment, HR, and marketing, that want to be seen as regular winners and who, through maintaining their winner's title related to an award, are able to showcase that they have maintained their performance level.

Other awards may have a 'win once' rule where they encourage new entrants – you may, however, be allowed to win a different category within the same awards.

Create an Awards Calendar

Finding the right sorts of awards to enter can be time-consuming, but the good news is that most are an annual occurrence. This means that rather than having to do the leg work each year to find awards, you should build yourself a calendar that includes the details, due dates, etc.

This calendar can be added to as and when you find new awards every year, as you will be able to simply follow the calendar and enter them as they arise in plenty of time. A calendar allows you to be prepared, giving yourself enough time to plan ahead and write a good entry without having to rush. Adding into your calendar the outcome of the awards that you enter, and the comments (if you receive any), can also help you to improve and build upon your results from previous years.

Diarising your 'must enter' awards will make sure they are given priority and don't slip through the consciousness of a busy business.

Previous Winners Identify the Benefits

We asked previous winners to explain what the benefits have been of being an award winner.

Abi Purser:

> I believe there are lots of benefits from a personal and a business perspective. It's a huge personal boost for me every time we are shortlisted, and of course when we win. Longcroft is my baby – my business that I have nurtured from day one, when I began with the very first Luxury Cat Hotel in my back garden in 2010. And every time we succeed in winning an award, I still have to pinch myself, because it reminds me just how far I, and now my growing team, have come. Every time we attend an awards ceremony it's a chance to reflect and feel some appreciation for where

we've got to. I have met so many incredible entrepreneurs and like-minded business people from attending awards events, and you never really know what doors they could open for you. Other people will take notice when they see you winning a prestigious award – it can only add legitimacy and credibility to your brand.

Adeem Younis:

As an entrepreneur and philanthropist, I have always endeavoured to go above and beyond in every dimension of our work. Winning an award offers an objective recognition of the efforts and achievements that you and your team have accomplished. It allows you to be celebrated among your peers and benchmark your work among others in your industry.

Angela Hughes:

There are lots of benefits – enhanced brand, networking at the ceremonies where I've met lovely people, a good news story for social media, a boost to morale and pride in winning. The research and completing the application concentrates the mind on what has been achieved.

Anna Rabin:

The biggest benefit is being able to actively market the fact that I am now an award-winning lawyer, and this has given me greater credibility and kudos.

Catherine Gladwyn:

It all started from the nomination. It was a wonderful content opportunity and enabled me to speak to my existing audience and to reach a wider one. When I won, it enabled me to speak to my audience again by thanking them for their votes. I now use 'award-winning' in my marketing.

Darren Clark:

You are able to reach more people and show them that anything is possible if you believe in yourself and work hard, and being able to showcase that with an award really helps reach people.

James Eades:

Applying for awards is usually put on the bottom of the 'to-do' list when time is short, but it is very important as it not only gains you social proof, but the awards evenings are a wonderful opportunity to meet and network with fellow business owners in real life.

Jo Macfarlane:

Aside from the PR opportunities and attraction of new customers, award wins really lift the team. We've found that award wins give a huge boost to the team in terms of morale, confidence and affirmation. Sharing a win throughout the business really does boost productivity.

Julie Grimes:

Winning an award has benefitted us in three ways: first, to look at the inside of your business and evaluate everything from your service, procedures and of course your financials all in line with your goals. Second, new client enquiries – as they read about you in the press, etc, and third, a huge boost of self-confidence, especially if you are a business owner with no boss to get that appraisal or pat on the back from.

Laura Birrell:

Winning an award gives you credibility. I use my awards when I present to potential customers.

Lynn Stanier:

> Having never won anything in my life, the credibility gave me a huge lift and boosted my confidence to really believe in myself and my work for the first time.

Natasha Penny:

> Being a winner has boosted my confidence to become a stronger, more confident business woman able to recognise my worth and value. Awards put us in the public eye and let people know about us and what it is we do, along with the fact we do it well. We have definitely received new customers because of our award wins.

Rachel Spratling:

> It helps you stand out ahead of your competition. Most clients or customers want to work with people who have been recognised for the work they do within their industry.

Ray Dawson:

> Winning the award has been very beneficial in terms of recognition, credibility and raising awareness of our charity and the great work that we do. It has also shown our volunteers just how important they are and lifting their self-esteem in the process. It has helped us win funding bids too.

Sam Bramley:

> The award gave credibility to the business, and it set us apart from others in our industry.

Sam Gooding:

> It clearly helps from a promotional and marketing perspective to be seen as an award-winning business. The internal benefits are an appreciation of the hard work the employees put into the business to make it what it is.

Simon Crowther:

> Running a business is more competitive than ever, and we have found winning awards helped give us the edge over our competitors. They have certainly helped with our credibility and exposure, and have been fantastic networking opportunities. Having our work recognised and being seen as successful has showcased our industry reputation.

Simon Buck:

> First, by entering you have to have your house in order, your stats, your story and your performance – it forces good practice. Next comes potential exposure and PR. Then there is the awards ceremony, a great opportunity to mix with other like-minded businesses.

Tracey Smolinski:

> Being an award winner makes you stand out from the crowd, builds credibility, and the PR helps you market for your brand. The more awards you have, the more your trust and credibility grows. If you were up against competitors, and you are an award winner and they are not, you have more chance of winning the business.

Gathering Evidence Before Writing the Award

You now know where to find awards and have developed a target list of awards you want to win. You have even added them to your diary to commit the time to their entry. The next part of the process is the planning and research stage. Yes, it does sound a bit heavy going but you do need to do it for success; and we don't mean success as a singular activity, but a good robust process that will give you a method for repeatable success.

Within the planning and research stage for your target awards, you do need to complete an evidence gathering exercise, because many of the questions you will be asked will need to be cross-referenced back to 'proof points' showing that these outcomes occurred.

First off, when you are entering awards (this sounds really obvious but is often avoided), read the instructions! It is worth noting that they may be presented across different areas of the entry process, with rules sometimes printed as part of the entry form, and possibly supplemental information contained within the terms and conditions, or cross-referenced on the entry website. Make sure you understand and read them all and cross-check the different bits of information, so you have a full understanding of what is required.

As part of this initial process, you really want to check that you are eligible. If it says for the 'startup' award you must have started trading after a stated date, you will be eliminated from the judging process because they will know when your business started. The award panel may use independent data verification such as checking records at Companies House, so they can find out when the company was registered or check your credit rating. If it is the case that you had a dormant company and you have only recently started trading with it, acknowledge that fact in your entry and state that although you registered the company at this point, it was dormant until you started trading at a named date – that way, it clarifies the situation. Make sure you are eligible or ask the question before you expend effort on your entry.

It may sound obvious, but many people rush into writing an entry and end up being caught out in terms of eligibility, criteria or word count further down the line. You will not be eligible for every award. If you fail to read and understand the eligibility criteria, you will waste hours of time that could have been spent on an award you *are* eligible for, instead of one that gets you nowhere.

It is always worth checking the marking scheme as well, alongside the response question structure. Those running the awards want to help you succeed in completing the entry correctly, and they will often have hints from the judges. These might be a top 10 list of hints and tips or even videos where the judges have uploaded a clip of what they are looking for. When they state what they really like to see – take notice!

Certain awards will also publish comments from the judges on previous winners – read and digest these to see how your business fits against the stated criteria.

Can you provide all the required information? In some cases, the award entry process may request your trading accounts, they might want a business plan or a training matrix. If they are asking you for that specific information, they will want to see it as it forms part of the judging process. You must make the informed commercial decision as to whether you are prepared to make that data public. If your business plan has a five-year strategy that includes the tactics you're going to employ, and you have to disclose it in the judging process, be conscious of the commercial sensitivity that information contains.

> We did hear from the judge of one award that someone refused to submit one of the pieces of data because they weren't happy about the confidentiality. Now they didn't submit the data, so they scored zero on that section, so they could not win. It is that transparent. If you don't want to reveal the data, don't enter that specific award. You must look at what the judging criteria are and what you are prepared to reveal about your future business direction. It is also worth acknowledging that a lot of account and trading information is readily available in the public domain.

Most awards are not purely 'past' facing, they will be looking at the history of what you have done but will also be interested to understand your dreams and aspirations for the future. You need to choose how much you reveal. The judges most often look at the direction of travel rather than the minute detail of specifics.

Among the criteria for entry might be a stated word count or page limit for the response. There are others that have no stated conditions, but you need to give the response justice in the detail delivered. If the entry rules say, for example, that there is a 1000-word response required, then you want to target 950 words minimum because they have given you a measure of what they expect to see. Word limits allow entries to be judged comparatively, and also, set the scale of the judging task to a fixed limit.

There may be other variations on the criteria whereby the whole entry submission has an overall page or word count limit, and you need to choose how you divide the scale of response to each of the questions. In this instance, you could be asked to respond to eight elements in an overall page-limited response. For these types of entries, the editing phase is essential, as you want to include as many examples as possible within the allowable space.

On a rarer occasion, specifically when you need to complete your entry online via a webpage, you might encounter a character count limit. These are common for online portals and often show a countdown of remaining characters as new information is entered. Character counts are harder to judge on how many words you have used, as it depends on the complexity of the language and length of words chosen. Succinctness is key.

No matter what the entry form structure, we always recommend that you generate your entry offline first. Put it in Word or in an email and save several copies to avoid any information losses. In Word you can then spell and grammar check, you can reformat, and you can confirm the word or character limit. Please don't type directly into a web portal as you run the risk of losing it if the website refreshes or internet access is interrupted. Many portals do have a Save function as you are developing the response, but we recommend that you don't chance it!

> We know someone who lost their whole entry of typed data when they added it straight to the website rather than putting the information into a separate document first. It was close to the deadline and they felt they could never phrase their entry as well again in a second attempt.

> Don't let that be you!

> After that happened, they felt totally demoralised and abandoned the entry process. This was now an award that they could not win, and the experience had a very negative impact on their award entries in the future.

Once you have an entry you are proud of and have saved, you can then upload it into the portal in plenty of time before the closing date. Do be aware that many people could be uploading very close to the deadline so don't leave it too late. Submit your entry in plenty of time to allow for any discrepancies between character or word count limits between the Word file and those of the portal. If there is a conflict, you will have time to edit the text to adhere to the website's stated limits. Read your entry and breathe in the normal places – does it have a natural pace and flow? If you are out of breath, then your sentences are too long. Shorter sentences make the content easier to read.

What are the entry rules? Do you understand them all? They may expect a commitment to come to a judging event, or expect you to host a visit at your premises to explain your entry in more detail, or to meet your staff and see your product or service in action. Know the rules and decide you are going to work within them before starting the process. We have mentioned earlier in the "Be

Aware – Not All Awards Are Created Equal" section that some awards expect you to attend the finalists' dinner as a prerequisite of being awarded your finalist status. So, you need to decide whether you want to enter under those rules. Most awards do not have any preconditions, and many award winners are recognised regardless of whether they attend, however, if the glory is due to you, of course you want to be there to accept the recognition in person.

If you have any doubts, it's always better to email the organisers expressing your interest in entering and stating your circumstance to confirm acceptability. Maybe a friend or colleague can attend on your behalf, ask the question first, then make that judgment call.

Most entries will require supporting evidence of some kind. Have you got a library of delighted client testimonials? Do you ask for feedback forms to be completed or reviews left? Look at the entry process and understand what extra evidence is required. Sometimes they want media coverage, sometimes they want client feedback. Case studies are often used to highlight a given project or service delivered – don't forget the importance of photos or, if you are feeling brave, video testimonials. The judges like to see people in action within their business environment. Make sure you capture these 'evidence points' when they occur throughout the year and amass them as a part of that process. We bet you will be surprised by the things you accomplished in a year.

This highlights another important aspect of award entry – that the process of the entry facilitates a meaningful review of your business. You can see how far you have come and how much the business has evolved and developed.

So before getting down to the writing of the application for the award, you'll need to take time to research the facts, figures and information that will help you win a particular category. For example, if you have entered the 'Best Innovation' category, you need to be looking for evidence that you can use to demonstrate specifically innovative aspects of your business. It might be that you've launched an innovative new app or customer service process that has made a real difference to your bottom line or customer satisfaction. It's not enough to simply say: "We have launched a new app that has improved the business's bottom line." You will need to provide facts and information about the app itself, including solid figures covering turnover and profits before and after the inception of the app, as well as customer numbers/reach. These must demonstrate in detailed, inarguable fact, how your business is innovative.

While it may be time-consuming to research this information, and you will need to talk to a number of people, the payoff will be worth it.

If you can, try to engage third party companies or people to support your entry. This can be in the form of clients who might provide you with a testimonial, as well as suppliers and partners who you might work with or have worked with in the past. It might be that you're a café that uses particular producers – if you have a good working relationship with them, see if they would write you a testimonial explaining how your work with them is helping them to grow and succeed.

Award judges will not simply take your word for it that your business is the best and should win. They want hard evidence – facts, statistics and testimonials of the benefits you have achieved for the business, your employees and society. Judges like before and after data, and quotes from third parties, especially those who have benefitted from the work you have done.

Remember though to provide all relevant detail in the entry itself – copy and paste it in or attach it as another document or image (if that is what is required). Don't hyperlink to anything as not every judging panel will have online copies – many work from paper copies, nor will they necessarily click on them if they have not asked for hyperlinks.

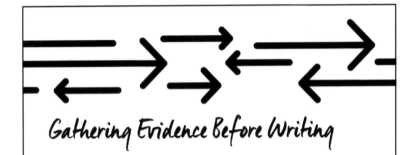

Gathering Evidence Before Writing

Read the instructions thoroughly:

- Check you are eligible?

- Can you provide all required information?

- Is there a stated word count or page limit?

- Do you understand all the entry rules?

- What extra evidence do you need to provide to support your entry?

  - Accounts

  - Case studies

  - Testimonials

  - Photos

Focus on Tailoring Your Entries

Each award is likely to be judged individually, so we would always recommend that you tackle each award independently. In the rules there is likely to be criteria that is specific to any one classification, and you need to make sure that your response is relevant and targeted.

Because the key to winning awards is in meeting and exceeding the criteria as best you can, every award entry must be bespoke and tailored in content and language to match the award category you are entering. Do not think that you can simply write one award entry for all the separate awards you want to enter; they need to be individually written. This may mean you have to enter fewer awards than you might like, but you will have a greater chance of winning those that you do enter. Quality trumps quantity when it comes to winning awards.

> Just like we advise our bid writing clients: 'Treat each award entry as a bespoke marketing campaign.' It is after all a promotional document about your business.

There is sometimes a single entry form that can be used to apply for multiple categories – in all likelihood, you will be asked to select a possible three from the list provided. With an entry of this format, you will need to answer and promote the aspects of the entry type you are focused on.

It might be the case that there are several awards you could be eligible for, but we suspect you will be able to identify a favourite that is the primary one. If you want to enter several awards, the core of your entry may be repeatable across different categories, enabling your master entry to be 'tweaked' to make it fit the others. However, you will need to recognise that there may be different marking agendas for each award, and possibly different judges. So, look at the stated criteria and be sure your response can match that classification.

In order to write bespoke answers, you will need to have very specific information at hand that reflects your points exactly. For example, if you are going for the 'Apprenticeship Provider of the Year Award' you would need to have testimonials from past apprentices, details of the amount of time they spent with your business, where they went, what happened to them upon completing their apprenticeships, etc. You might also like to include feedback from the college or institution that is providing the apprentices, the figures that show how your apprentices have benefitted, your business's finances – you get the idea! The information you would need for this entry would be very different from the information you might need to provide for Innovative Business of the Year or Environmentally Friendly Business of the Year. Focus is key.

So, treat each award individually, read the criteria that the judges will mark your entry against and research and find evidence appropriately to match the requirements.

How do you find the information that is key to unlocking award success? You will want to find the unique details that can enhance your entry, so you need to understand where that knowledge is held. Is there anybody within your business you can interview to provide specific information? You will need to extract the specifics – the facts and figures that back up the dialogue of the story. If you can tap into someone's knowledge and experience, you can gain different views and perspectives that add richness and variety to the entry.

You will need this evidence. The judges want to be able to see tangible reasons and benefits delivered, quantified with real life stories. A single viewpoint will get you a certain distance, but an endorsement from other members of your team, a client or a student will be so much more powerful, engaging and influential.

Use those facts and figures, show turnover as a percentage and a figure, show growth year on year, make a graph out of it. Anything that makes the data more interesting to the eye.

Don't simply recycle old information wholesale from one year to another, or from one award to another. Please make use of key facts and endorsements and make sure you refer to the award you are entering by name (and don't leave in the name of the old award you just copied). The worst thing for anybody assessing an entry is when a previous different award name has been left in by mistake. Not only does it show you have just cut and pasted, it shows a lack of attention to detail which is not going to endear you to the judges and get your name on that award.

You must recognise that because the judging criteria are so different across the various awards, the chances are, what you wrote for one won't have the focused journey and storytelling that is aligned to the judging criteria of the next award. We would recommend that you can keep all your key facts and attributes in a separate document so, when you are ready to enter a specific award, you can then plan the story around your 'win themes' and add in your facts to make it individual and bespoke to that specific award entry.

Debbie Gilbert acknowledges: "Award entries often ask similar questions, and they might not alter too much in subsequent years. Once you have a good body of information, you can then tweak in the future."

As we have recommended previously, we believe that you need to start the evidence and collation process early. Up-to-date information is essential, especially the statistics associated with your company and the personal stories. When you have identified your awards target list, you will know which ones you want to do, and having researched them, will understand when they will open for entry and what the application criteria are.

It has to be recognised that some awards require more ongoing effort than others, which have an amazing and potentially time-consuming spread of activity. The benefit of this ongoing process is that there is an enhanced level of engagement and more opportunities to promote your business.

The latter type might have a prelaunch event, then an actual timeline of the entry, then the meet the judge's event, then an assessment event, all before the winner is announced at the awards ceremony. This can involve a large amount of interaction over an extended time period. The resource requirement should form part of your assessment at the evidence gathering stage – make sure that you can commit to the entirety of the process.

It makes sense that you review the 'how to enter' videos online alongside any tips from the judges. There may be interviews with previous winners that provide great insight. Research those historic entries and see who the previous winners were, learn from what they share. Many awards have their own websites with content featured that might go back several years. You can see which businesses won, and the specific themes they were looking for from their finalists and ultimate winners.

These sites usually provide very specific hints and tips, especially the large national awards and those promoted by industry bodies. Read around the entries, are they looking to promote business growth or scaling up, or are they looking to reward innovation? You will need to understand the criteria they are looking for. Do your homework, interview people in your business who can provide those important facts and figures and look to the awards resource history to understand what successful businesses have done in the past.

If you are writing applications for awards on behalf of your company and you are not the owner of the business, you will need to ensure that you interview and talk to as many relevant people as possible. Not only will this provide the current facts and figures, it may also bring to your attention an important point that could have been otherwise overlooked. Talk to department heads, the CEO (if possible), the finance department, etc. The more people you talk to, the more valuable evidence you will be able to gather that can be weaved into your answers. This will help you avoid the waffling used due to the lack of solid information.

Roni commented on what she has learned through the entry process: "You have just got to be honest about what you have done and sell yourself in terms of what you have achieved. I write from the heart when I fill the forms out and don't have specialist advice or have entries written for me."

Caroline points out the need to carefully read the questions and answer them as accurately as possible without going off on a tangent. "You really have to study the questions and answer them accurately. It's important to include as much quantitative information as possible. Show what you have achieved through numbers, prove how you have grown. Increasingly, there is a steer toward wanting to understand your corporate social responsibility, environmental factors and community involvement.

Although they want to see that you are growing and sustaining a profitable business, I think there are other things that have come much more into the mix, such as what we have done to support our local community and our environmental policy in action in the office. It's a combination of those things, but the most important is just reading the questions really carefully and making sure you answer them to the best of your ability."

Activity

- Identify the main stories associated with your business.

- Capture key client testimonials – which ones will you include?

- What have you delivered that you think is outstanding?

Writing Skills

Following the evidence gathering stage, you now have lots of great facts and figures, and it's time to write your entry. You will need to pull all of this information together in a compelling, interesting and winning way.

Writing award entries is no quick task, even after you have spent time on the planning and research stage. Being concise and informative while ensuring your entry reflects the category criteria without waffling, takes time, effort and skill.

When you are drafting your entry, the first thing we recommend, even before the technicality of the writing, is to appreciate effective time management. Look at the structure of the response required and split your effort and time into those elements. What does the question structure state in terms of what the expected response needs to be to match it? If you are being asked for 10 individual responses, create your structured reply into those 10 parts and divide up your time by those 10 parts. If you believe that each portion requires an hour to create the response, then allow yourself an hour for each part. If it is 10 minutes for some and an hour for others, scale your effort accordingly. Make sure you have allotted the time relative to the level of detail required.

When you have calculated the time needed to complete the entry, work back from the submission date. This will allow you to understand the latest point it is reasonable to start, but make sure you allow time for other activities in between as your usual working and private life will have to continue. If you have got a good idea of how long it will take you to generate the response, you know the point at which the submission must be made and what the magnitude of the commitment is alongside the rest of your agenda.

You will have already read the rules of engagement and know what is expected for the whole entry process. This is very important as it is natural to stall on a more difficult question, and you will certainly start off answering the easier questions as you will have more confidence in generating the response. How you set off will depend on how you like to work – do you like to 'eat the frog' and get the difficult ones out of the way first? Do you prefer to build your momentum and get the simple responses sorted first? There is no right or wrong answer. Work the way that suits you best in order to get to the result. Remember you are developing a story and your entry is taking the reader on a journey. With this in mind, make sure all the themes build on each other, making logical progress through your written entry.

It makes sense to identify the subject matters you have the most information on as these will be easier and quicker to 'talk about'. Most respondents are happy to chat about the company history with confidence but find it trickier to explore some of the softer subjects such as explaining what community engagement activities have been undertaken. The social and community aspects of your business are likely to feature highly in any award submission. Judges want to know what you do outside the normal tasks of the business that are delivered to paying clients. They may be keen to understand your sustainability agenda, what you deliver on training and how you actively retain your staff.

All of the questions asked will need to be addressed, and if you are on a tight time deadline, this will become much trickier. So, make sure you read through all the questions first and split the requirements of what you need to deliver into time chunks that are relevant for you to complete. We would never recommend that you rely on time extensions to the submission date. Some awards will do them as a matter of course, and others will never extend the deadline for entry. If you have an issue with completing the entry on time, you can always contact the organisers and request a time extension, but the rules are published for everyone to abide by, so don't expect that this will always happen.

While an unexpected deadline extension may work to your advantage, as you may get the chance to include some additional data, you may alternatively be left feeling disappointed if you pushed other things aside to concentrate on the entry. We expect that your diary is full, and your days are busy regardless of the awards you are entering, so it is far better to keep a positive attitude and see if there is anything you can add now that you've been granted a bit more time. If you truly believe that you did your best with the resources you had, within the time that was available to you, then congratulations on getting the form submitted – there is nothing more that can be expected.

If you do end up having a bit more time, you can choose to finesse your answers, or you can recognise that your entry is the best you could do. Unless you have got some great new data, or a lovely new testimony, or an additional story to tell, save your effort and focus on your next target award. If you have up-to-date accounting figures, these are always worth including as they provide the best current reflection of the business's financial status.

There are shortcuts you can develop to help you understand how much time it will take to complete the entry. Time yourself and see how long it takes you to generate a response of 500 words, for example. If there are word limited responses, you can then estimate your time to complete all the questions and have a good idea of how much time it is going to take.

Recognise that you are unlikely to manage a whole day of drafting responses – instead make yourself diary slots of one or two hours, or even half an hour. Schedule these during the identified timeframe you have allocated to concentrate solely on drafting the entry. It is easy to get sucked into looking at emails, answering calls or browsing the internet. Making your writing time an official diary appointment can really help you deliver effective time management.

It is important to identify within the writing process, scheduled time for drafts and revisions as well. Within your planned timeline, allow another trusted person to independently proofread what you have created. If you are using an awards entry writing agency or a copywriter to help you write it, they are likely to have jobs booked in advance so they can schedule the various drafts and allow time for approval before the deadline.

Whomever you have involved in your writing process, you will potentially need data from other people or other sources, such as your accountant, to support the entry. Schedule those dates well within the planning structure so you will have plenty of time for the entry to do your business justice.

Many of the large national awards that are more intense to enter actually have quite a large time window, as they appreciate the depth of the process for the entrants. For example, the Great British Entrepreneur of the Year Awards open in mid-March and close at the end of June. The organiser will see a peak of entries just after entry opens, pulses of responses based on promotional activity and then a massive uplift in entries just before the deadline.

You may be the person who likes to get it done quickly at the beginning of the entry window, but there is also the recognition that for small businesses a lot can change in a week, let alone three months! You may therefore choose to draft your entry early in the process but add in the latest financial projections and testimonials nearer the end of the entry timeline. You will want to ensure that the entry is as relevant as you can make it, so it might be that you can respond to the history questions and then draft the current challenges responses nearer the end.

Our successful entry in the Great British Entrepreneur of the Year Awards was done near the deadline. So much was changing in the business at the time, so we wanted to make sure that we included the most current information. This included the fact we had just helped a client to win a major bid. Add in the new information as soon as it is available, and your entry will then present the most up-to-date picture of your business.

It is true to say that it's easier to critique than to create. We know that to be universally true from our extensive experience in bid writing. It is a human instinct that you can spot errors within detail but getting the information on to the page to start with can be difficult. A good writer needs to be able to gather information, understand the significance and impact and then develop a focused response. The same principles need to be applied to a good award entry. What sounds simple is in fact a very specific skill set – procuring information and looking for what is relevant, putting the data into a structure, telling a story, and then evolving all the messaging into the final response. It is also a journey that involves a fair amount of iteration – not all the answers are there at the beginning. You may need to revisit the response to a question that doesn't feel right and edit it, or perhaps completely reformat it.

The chances are that you won't have the best and final version of your entry on the first attempt. To maximise the chance of winning with the best entry that you can generate, you will need to get your thoughts down on paper as a first stage, and then revisit your content and structure afterwards to assess it. Be brave, allow someone else to review it and challenge the information. An independent proofreader has another advantage apart from the fact you become word blind to your own errors as you see what you want to see, not what's actually there. That is because you know the story of your business too well. This impartial person will be able to clarify and question the information provided so you can be clear on the benefit. If you are able to debate the content and agree on the outcome, the entry will be much stronger for it.

We would also recommend that you give your proofreader the entry criteria, so they can judge your response by reviewing against it. Someone who did not work on the entry can have an unbiased view and might be able to add detail you have overlooked, as well as check the logic of the journey as you are presenting the story of your business.

Roni provided this excellent advice: "Speak from the heart, tell your journey in your own way."

You will need to harness your writing skills to make your entry stand out. How do you do that? Well, you need to showcase the unique aspects in your business and highlight the benefits they deliver in your application. Yes, not all aspects will be unique, but it is likely the way they are packaged and delivered are.

Marketers speak of USPs – Unique Selling Points. This is how you need to think about your company – not only about what is unique and special, but specifically the way that this drives sales for your company.

When presenting your business on the entry form, you will need to identify the things that will make you stand out, so you need to know what they are! Make sure you play to your strengths when writing an award entry. It is not the time to be bashful – but groundless boasting won't do you any good either. All the content needs to be framed within the benefit delivered to customers.

Good news sells, but it doesn't all have to be what went well. Include things that didn't go according to plan, as this can make your entry far stronger. It shows the journey you have been on and the learning that you captured. Recovering from a failure, detailing what you have learned and how you will change going forward is a huge strength in showcasing the education gained from the experience.

If you want to stand out, you will need to exhibit what you can give that others can't. You will need to acknowledge specifically what makes you stand out. Do you have a particular niche? Have you created a trading model that is new to the market? Is it that you are in a rural area and have given the chance to staff to work part-time, or perhaps you have given a training opportunity to someone who has been denied opportunities in the past? You might have a specialised solution or a sector of knowledge that nobody else can replicate. Are clients delighted to find you because you are able to provide something to them that they have not been able to experience before? How has that brought additional value to them? You will need to explain why it is a benefit.

Knowing what you do well is one thing, but you need to think about quantifying your evidence. Judges also love to see innovation. Have you created a new way of doing something? An extension to a range? A more convenient delivery method? Show what it was, detail why you added this to your offer and explain why the innovation was valuable. You might have transferred some learning from your previous experience into a new context, or perhaps you have gained knowledge from a previous part of your life that you have applied to a new scenario. If no one has thought of it before in the way you are delivering it, then it is innovation.

Don't be shy – you need to be telling the story of the who, when, what and the how of your business, so you are setting the scene for the judges to understand how great you are.

> Before I had a career in marketing, and prior to the internet, I loved to enter consumer competitions. Of special interest to me were the 'slogan types', those with the requirement to complete a sentence in a nominated number of words. You had to state why you wanted to win, or why a given product was the best. Little did I know in my teens that I was helping create marketing messages for these companies. Translating

their benefits into slogans was excellent training for my future marketing career. I would normally buy the qualifiers – usually a product from the promoter, keeping the receipt to send as proof of purchase. This was then included with the paper entry form and after answering a few questions which were designed to be simple to complete, the effort was then spent on the slogan, which was the element of skill demanded by the competition rules.

I won many prizes, from trips to New York, to a day as a jeweller where I designed my own pendant. Sharing information was key and formed the thesis of my BA degree – collaboration in competitive environments.

I was part of a newsletter group who would save entry forms we found, mostly in the supermarkets, and then post them on to each other. Yes, we were competitors, but we also realised that by each of us encouraging others to enter, we were also making the competitions themselves more successful. This in turn would encourage more companies to run them and give us more chances to win in the future.

There are still many 'compers' who have a great time winning prizes in consumer competitions from cars to holidays, electrical appliances to garden tools. It was a fabulous hobby that turned out to be a magnificent education.

Writing Skills

- Be innovative – demonstrate your value

- What will make you stand out?

- Play to your strengths

- Tell your story – What, Who, When and How

- What can you give that others can't?

Activity

- What are your USPs?

- What innovative services or products have you delivered?

- Which clients are you going to approach for testimonials?

Your Entry Is A Marketing Campaign

When crafting your awards entry, you need to treat it as a one-off, bespoke and tailored marketing campaign. That of course is truly what it is – the chance to market your business in a focused output. If you were promoting yourself in the format of a traditional campaign, you would have your objectives, timetable, budget and a target outcome. Award writing is like that. It is a form of promotion that involves communication skills in the language that you use. It involves connection, identifying what is most relevant to your audience, and it involves showing value, by offering proof that what you delivered was of benefit to your clients. The target outcome is the recognition of winning the award.

The award entry process is a focused proposal. It is the pitch to the judges of why you should be selected from all those who entered.

You are selling what the benefit of your business is, but be mindful to do that at the final stage of the journey. What are you more convinced by, a salesperson who says, "I'm great here's why" or a story where the benefit is revealed, and you can make up your own mind?

Most people understand that telling the story of your business builds an emotional connection. Humans are influenced, and ultimately buy, based on emotions first, we then support this with logic in the decision making. If the judges feel an emotional connection to your entry and the story you are telling, they will bond with your content and feel positively toward your submission.

Don't brag. We all know people who say how good they are, yet if we are honest, we have trouble believing them. So, doesn't it make sense to get your clients and employees to say how great your business is? This is why including testimonials in your entries is so powerful and so much more influential. Let other people talk on your behalf. It is like a conversation with several tones and accents – it's a far richer endorsement than any amount of self-promotion.

When scripting your response for the award entry, you need to be aware of the tone and positivity of the language used. Your award entry needs to read as if you want to win. That involves the use of 'benefits-led messaging'. When you are writing your entry, you should be using upbeat language. You need to highlight why you undertook certain actions and what benefits were delivered as an outcome. Think as if you are reading it aloud. You really don't want it to be dull and monotone, it needs to be enthusiastic and varied in pace – like the delivery of a good story. Remember to quantify the benefits that you have delivered, on an emotional as well as a practical level.

Show your business values, and how you are consistent and true to them. Then back that up with a client who said you were great and can explain what the value delivered to them was. Knowing that you made a difference is the biggest accolade you can have in your business.

> One of the most powerful quotes we were able to add to an entry was from a client where our bid writing was instrumental in saving a nearly 100-year-old company.

> "I would like to take this opportunity to thank you – you have been a good friend to us, and your bid writing has almost certainly saved our company, you are part of our family." Neil Griffiths, W B Griffiths and Son.

> The testimonial was so powerful it was read out in the judges' comments – find a quote that is as powerful for your business.

Remember in this context that the judges are your target audience. Prepare as much as possible and keep looking for signals of what the assessors might be looking for. If the awards involve a meet the judges event, always try to attend or at least engage and say how sorry you are that you can't be there and share social media content instead. Find out from the judges what is on their agenda and follow their social media feeds, as well as the actual award entry website, as this is a great place to determine the vision and values of those who are assessing. Find out what they view as most important – do they really want to know that you are recruiting someone locally? Do they want to know you have offered training? Or are they interested in your innovation or ability to export? Is there an event hashtag#? Use this to cross-reference your commentary.

Spell Out the Benefits You Deliver

You need to be able to detail the specific benefits of your approach within your business. This will allow the judges to understand what sets you apart. There might arguably be several other businesses that can do what you do, other accountants, pet trainers, hairdressers, construction companies or business coaches, and unless you are in a totally new space that nobody has ever been in before, you will have to stand out above your peers. In fact, being an innovative business in a totally new space presents its own challenge of explaining what you do, and what the benefit is as the judges won't have anything to compare it to.

Your competition will not just be those in the same profession, but also potentially those that compete for the same customer spend, such as a hotel offering mini breaks, competing with a jeweller for a gift occasion.

Every business has various forms of competition, so you need to understand and identify what sets you apart. Is it that you are flexible and adaptable? Is it that you'll drop everything and help clients 24/7? Is it that you have got knowledge of large organisation processes that you can share with smaller ones that wouldn't have that knowledge and exposure otherwise? Can you apply learning from one market sector or client type to a different one or another area of the country?

Think about what your existing clients love about you and why they value it so much. Do you know what it is? Have you asked your clients what they love about you? It would certainly be worth doing a survey to ask them, as you will keep updated with their preferences and attitude toward your business. Customer satisfaction surveys are also excellent evidence to include.

Replicate the language, tone and format used in your award entry writing to show others why your current customers cherish what you bring to their relationship. Frame the benefits in terms and phrases associated with the specific expectations of the award type. So, if the award is looking for innovation, you will need to show how the innovation you deliver has practical benefits for your clients.

If the award is focused on business leadership, you will need to structure your response to maximise that aspect; how the vision for the business has united all the employees or how the charisma of the leader has made for an engaging speaker. The awards may be targeted at a specific industry, in which case they will be looking for attributes that are valued within that area of expertise that provide tangible worth. Always keep the judges central to your benefits-led messaging structure, make it easy for them to understand why this is of value and how it can be replicated for new clients in the future.

Present the best version of your business so you can be judged on your positivity and make sure you look good on that piece of paper or electronic portal. You cannot guarantee that the person judging the entry has any prior knowledge of your business, and for national and international classifications this becomes much less likely. For regional awards you are more likely to be known to the judges especially if you have a high profile and have built a reputation. The important point to note is this – they can't judge you unless you have included the details for that specific entry. Many judges have made the comment that "we know this is a good business, but their entry did not do them justice." Don't let that apply to your business. Make your strengths clear, and back them up with evidence and testimonials. Highlight why you should be the winner by giving the judges multiple sources of evidence to confirm that they have made the correct choice to select you as a winner.

Writing award entries can be hard work for those not comfortable in the process. Make it easier for yourself the next time by avoiding having to go unnecessarily through activities multiple times. Develop some sort of a filing structure that works for you and create an information hierarchy so you can easily search for previous entries and the relevant content within them. Develop the structure of your story and the win themes that are focused on your company.

This is of specific value when you are asked similar questions: "Why did you start the business?" and "What is the business history?" Reviewing past entries allows you to see the evolution in your writing. With feedback on past entries, you should be able to identify what worked and impressed the judges. You also need to know the specific areas of weakness that need to be addressed. When you have a filing hierarchy, you will be able to search for keywords that will help develop future nominations. Create a library so you have all content of that subject matter filed in the same place. You might use a CRM (Customer Relationship Management) system, or you may prefer to put it into a Word document. There are constantly evolving apps and programs that can help. The main point is to keep the information up-to-date in whatever format works best for you.

In this situation evidence really does matter. Everything must show what you have or can do with the tangible evidence to prove the fact.

Debbie comments: "No one likes a Rich Tea! Make your business nice and interesting, show your passion, make it attractive."

When asked what they included within their winning entries, Caroline, Gaby and Roni had the following advice:

Caroline and Gaby:

> I think to show that you have an accurate handle on your finances and incorporate the last three years of finances. Include your growth percentages instead of just the numbers. Read the questions really accurately. It's always good to get a second pair of eyes on the entry because there are sometimes things that have been missed, and our MD will normally come back with his feedback. Definitely get somebody else who is knowledgeable about the business to look at the application.

If the awards ask for supporting material then certainly use a business growth plan and submit visual aids so the judges can get a feel for your brand. Also include details about your business working with charities in the community. We always include as much imagery as we can, ideally if there is a video that showcases the company then it's always worth including that as well.

Roni:

I think it's important to flag up everything that you do. So rather than just saying I am passionate about engineering, say how and why you are passionate about engineering. Explain exactly what you are doing and give examples. Talk about your extra-curricular activities too.

The 5 Ws of Winning

The 5 Ws of award entry can be whatever you want, the trick is to create something that you can remember and apply! Our preference for the 5 Ws have the same rules we use for networking, and as expected it is the fifth W that is the one that gives you standout. To be successful in your award entry process you will need to quantify the What, Who, When and Where of your business, because that will encompass all the elements with quantifiable evidence. It is this proof that makes your entry strong, because you have captured data and have the reinforcement of what was actually delivered, backed by testimonials to prove it.

Winning would also make a worthy fifth W, but our final one is, 'What's in it for me?' That's where you explicitly state what your customer gains from what you offer, and where you highlight what your clients actually want from you. If the customers can see the benefit then the judges will as well! You need to give them a compelling reason as to why you should be judged as the winner, just like a client wants to know what benefit you will deliver to them.

You have already written your entry in the language of 'What's in it for me?' as you have used benefits-led messaging and quantified this for your audience, so the judges will already understand what advantage you are providing to them. Remember on the entry form that the judging panel is seeing your business through the eyes of a client, so the more testimonials and evidence you can provide to showcase your claims, the greater trust and worthiness your entry will have.

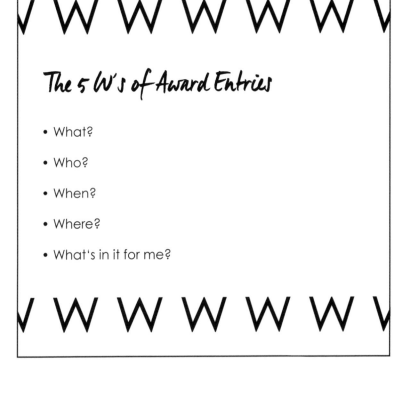

The 5 W's of Award Entries

- What?
- Who?
- When?
- Where?
- What's in it for me?

Offline Then Online

We have said this before but will repeat it as it is very important – before inputting your entry into any online format, we highly recommend that you develop your response offline first. The disaster of having an internet crash when you are at the end of your entry and you have not yet written everything somewhere else is just too terrible to comprehend and may result in you abandoning the entry.

There is sometimes the opportunity to save the application and return to it later, but this is not always the case. It is often impossible to complete a good award entry in one sitting. Therefore, we would always advise anybody writing awards to write out their answers in a Word document before copying and pasting the finished articles into the relevant boxes on the application form. This allows you to return again and again to your work, as well as send it off to colleagues or friends to proofread and check.

By creating the offline version in a program such as Word first, you can keep a copy as your entry progresses. This gives you a structure that you can edit, spell and grammar check, and where you can use the read aloud function to hear what your response sounds like. Another advantage to this way of working is apparent if there are word or character limits, as you will be able to edit to meet the requirements and understand how much content you are able to present in your response. You also have the chance to email your work to a trusted colleague who can see what you have written before the commitment of the actual entry submission.

When creating the content offline, you do need to be aware of the word or character counting mechanism and how it works. It is not uncommon for online applications to use word counts or even character counts that differ slightly from word processing packages. You need to acknowledge that not all counting mechanisms are the same. When submitting your edited entry via the awards website page, you may get an alert that you need to lose a few words. It is never very much, but if you are at the limit of the maximum word count, which we always recommend, you will need to take this into consideration. If this is the case, go back to your original, make your edits and put it back into the portal to make sure you optimise the response.

Most awards will have guidelines and criteria that entrants need to follow. Often, every question will have a word limit which you *must* stick to – if they ask for 500-word answers, give them 500-word answers. Going too far below the word count can suggest to them that you don't have enough to say or detailed evidence about how your business fits within the criteria. Going over the word count may disqualify you or suggest that you are waffling too much while failing to provide the important information. Both scenarios will negatively affect your entry and chances of success.

Whether the guidelines explicitly say so or not, it is expected that the award entrant in the category entered answers every question fully. In many awards there are questions to be answered that are the same in every category, alongside some category specific questions that will also need answering. It is vital that you answer both sets of questions to the best of your ability and ensure that even the generic question answers are still tailored to the category you enter. If you are entering an award for most innovative business of the year, for example, even the generic questions that ask about the history of your business will need to reflect your innovative nature and practise.

A lot of the time, portals allow you to download and extract the question structure. You can put this format into a different document such as a Word file, allowing you to compose all your answers. Then take the developed responses and add them back into the portal to complete.

Occasionally you may encounter a webpage where the form doesn't allow you to progress to the next question until you have populated the answer box. If this is the case, it may be challenging as you won't know what questions will be asked later in the process. This situation is unusual as, for the majority of the time, there will be a specific document presenting all the questions, enabling you to understand what is required. In this unlikely event, type a standard sentence into each response and get yourself through to the next stage, so you can see what is being asked. You should be able to get all the way through and not have to submit. When you are ready with your ideal response, the webpage format will let you over-type your answers.

Some portals allow multiple versions of the submission before the deadline. You will usually see a draft or version number, and you can keep editing your response and re-saving until the deadline. At this point, the last uploaded response would be the one passed to the judges. These are often date clocked to show they met the rules and were submitted prior to the deadline. Check out the entry rules – it should be clear what the instructions are.

Time is always the challenge – if you are time-strapped, and you want to get an entry in, we recommend that you 'upload a banker'. If you have had a chance to work on something and it's as close to finished as you can get it (in the imperfect world of never enough time and never enough money), get that submission in. The beauty of this approach is you know you have an entry 'in the bank', and what happens from here on in with your business life means you either will or won't get a chance to revisit it. But, you do have an entry submitted.

If the entry systems work on an over-write principle, you will have the option to make changes at a later date, and they will not be over-written until the moment you hit the Resubmit button. Once you have a submission in, you have a submission. You can edit later, but if you never have the chance to get back to it, you will still have a valid response in place.

Make sure you submit your entry on time – don't wait until a few minutes before the deadline if you can help it. Try to submit the day before, or at least with a few hours to spare, as this gives you enough time to deal with technical issues such as your computer crashing or your internet going down, otherwise all your hard work will be wasted. Also remember that once you have pressed Submit, you are not normally able to make any amendments to your entry.

It is important to choose the right person to craft your entry, and we use the word craft advisedly, as there is a skill to the language and response structure used. It might be that you want to hire a professional to help you write it, or you can ask friends or business colleagues that you know have good language skills to critique your entry. It does make sense to choose someone who knows about your business as they can make suggestions of additional things to include that you may have overlooked. However, it is imperative that you have selected someone who has the passion and enthusiasm for you to win.

While the head of department, accountant, lawyer or specific expert may have the facts and figures, they are not normally the best people to write an awards entry. Overly technical applications that are full of jargon and acronyms are difficult for judges to follow and understand, and they usually fail to communicate the strengths of your company well. Contrastingly, your PR and marketing department or person tend to have excellent communication skills. They know how to present complex information in the most compelling and engaging way – exactly what is needed for award success. They can easily liaise with or interview you, as the business owner, as well as the technically minded individuals in your business who will be best placed to provide the evidence.

If, following a review, the entry does not contain benefits-led messaging with a passionate compelling response, then it is going to be hard work to read and even harder to make it a winner. If the entry is factual but not compelling, even with an emotional connection, it is still unlikely to stand out against those that are engaging as well as exciting.

To optimise your submission success, write every award individually. Even consider how the same question may vary across given categories. Look to the judging notes to see what they are looking for, as they may require a slightly different answer. For example, innovation in a category may be different depending on the nuances that they have presented to you, so you do need to read the rules to understand what those differences are in the structure.

You may find that some awards have various categories that you would like to enter, or that there are multiple awards you are going to enter in a year. Either way, every single award or award category you enter requires a unique and bespoke approach in order to win. If you are entering two categories for one award, for example, Small Business of the Year and Innovation Business of the Year, both will require different answers to lots of the same questions. If asked for an example about business growth, the small business entry answer would focus on the growth of your business regarding employee size, customers and clients, turnover and products or services. The innovation category answer should also include the same sort of information, but the writing will be angled differently.

When talking about product and service growth, the Small Business of the Year answer would focus on the number of new products and services implemented throughout the year, but this would not be the main focus of the answer, unlike the Innovation Business of the Year answer, which would place a larger focus on the product and service offering. It will also talk about the growth in the business's technological understanding and innovation, and how this has had an effect on the growth of the business. The new technology may have attracted new customers, which has in turn meant increased demand and profit growth and the recruitment of additional employees. In contrast, for the small business, you would place a greater emphasis on the growth of your business, while allowing for new technological innovations.

Keep the award criteria in mind all the time that you are writing your entry. The judge will be reading your submission with the criteria beside them, so you need to excel at meeting the criteria, rather than simply listing your achievements.

How to Make Your Entry Stand Out

So how do you make your entry stand out above the others? The answer may depend on the format you need to submit in. It may be a portal with no option to add images, or an upload facility where you can add a document that you have created. When formatting, you have the option to use colours and imagery, and you will also need to write short and easy to read sentences that logically progress through the entry. There is a temptation when you are passing on knowledge, to write extended paragraphs of text or overly long sentences. If somebody has to draw breath three times when reading the sentence, then it is too long. You really want to make it snappy, so the assessment panel can retain that information.

Judges will be reading a lot of award submissions, which often blend into one. It is, therefore, important to make your submission stand out. While it's not always possible to use interesting colours or a lot of imagery, as answers may need to be entered in boxes on the application, you can make your answers stand out through your writing. Short, easy to read paragraphs, concise sentences with little waffle, and facts and figures backing up your points make reading an entry easy on the judge and thus, both easier to remember and favourable.

However, if you have the opportunity to upload a file containing your answers, then use the occasion to make your award entry eye-catching and interesting with colours, images, infographics, charts and graphs. A visually interesting entry is more likely to stay in the mind of the judge than huge chunks of text. It is important that you don't use visual aspects to try to cover up poor writing – your focus should be on making your answers concise and to the point, yet informative.

If you make your submission easy to read, it makes it easy for the judge to award you credit. Use headings and subheadings to structure your response in a consistent way, while obviously acknowledging and abiding by any page, word or character counts. The judges will appreciate that you have signposted them to how the response matches their assessment criteria. Graphs and tables are a great way to do this as they summarise information in an easy to consume manner. It is certainly true in this scenario that a picture paints a thousand words.

Make your entry easy to navigate, putting the most relevant and important information first. Judges have to read through a lot of applications, so the easier it is for them to find the information they need, the better your chances of success, and you avoid the risk of your entry's winning points being missed. Similarly, while visuals are good, they have to make sense at a glance, be relevant, appropriate, add value and have a clear purpose. Badly used graphs, diagrams and images can do more harm than good, so make sure there is a clear reason for yours being there.

Do you have a YouTube channel? Purpol have used this to great effect by uploading video testimonials from our interns and filming one of our intern strategy days so we could include it within an award entry.

Create a special message for the judges and include the URL and link within your form so they can view the message.

This shows thought and innovation, and they get to see you in action and speaking with your own voice as well.

Keep your writing simple yet practical and assertive. There are places where your language skills will be valued in terms of how many large words you can use, but this is only likely to be a benefit for academic or industry specific entries. Award entries generally need to be universally understood, so that means avoiding jargon and unexplained acronyms.

Jargon, unexplained acronyms and wordy, difficult sentences, make it hard for a judge to understand whether you are answering the question or fit the category criteria.

There may be a point that you want to include using industry specific language if you are in a technical world, or a given sector where those acronyms are well known. For example, in recruitment or finance there will be language that is useful and known to your cohorts. If you will be marked by judges who are in that area of specialism, they will know what you mean. But you do run the risk if you are talking in financial language and the person marking it is from HR or Sales, that they may not understand what you are describing, because they are unfamiliar with the phrases used.

If the award category is a universal award category such as entrepreneurship, for example, stick to widely understood business language as the judges will understand the terminology used, and you will not risk misinterpretation.

Ensure your answers focus on what the assessors are actually asking for. Similarly, you need to avoid using meaningless marketing speak. Award judges read a lot of entries and will, therefore, have seen every cliché. But don't place style over substance as an explanation in plain English is far better than wordy, technical sounding jargon that avoids getting to the point.

A good example to include could read like this: 'We should win Small Business of the Year because we have grown from a two-person business to a four-person business in the last 12 months, that is on track to turnover £180,000, exceeding our target of £150,000, achieving 50% of growth in the last year.'

Here is a vague, less impactful example: 'We should win this award because of our forward-thinking, innovative approach, and our emphasis on out-of-the-box thinking that's unique to our industry. Our specialist agency offers a holistic full-service solution.' As you will read, this uses a lot of words but does not actually mean anything definite to the assessor. The latter statement content is weak, providing no evidence of your business's success and warns the judge that you may be trying to hide behind technical language because of a lack of solid, positive evidence to support how your business fits the award criteria.

It is important to only provide information that the criteria has asked for – this will all be laid out in the guidance documents that come with the application form. Judges won't consider irrelevant information in their decision process, and you are wasting valuable words that could be used to explain how you fit the criteria.

Some of the simplest and most significant ways to ensure your entry is clear and easy to understand are through the use of bullet points, headings, subheadings and paragraphs. Large chunks of text are difficult to follow and make it easy for the judge to miss important points. When you have figures to list, don't list them in long sentences, bullet point them.

Even for uploads to a portal, you may have the opportunity to format the text. Make the information easy to digest by breaking up what is otherwise a solid series of text heavy paragraphs.

Write your response as an evolving story, ensuring that you cross-reference themes within the content as this will make your entry more cohesive. It will also embed the facts for the judges as they read it, showing the real benefits you have delivered. Avoid waffle and speak from the heart in an engaging way, just as you would if you were having a conversation.

You cannot, however, assume that all elements of an entry are read together, as experts are sometimes brought in to mark a specific element. This might be the case for a financial question where a judge with financial expertise is assessing the company accounts. What usually happens is that entries are judged by a panel, on the entirety of that entry, for that given category. That is why it's important for your business storytelling journey to unfold logically.

As part of your scoping process, we recommend that you develop win themes. These elements are the key facts of a central idea (features and benefits of your business delivery), acting as an overriding theme that you believe will showcase why you should win. These should form part of a compelling story, so you show several facets of the benefits you have delivered. The win theme is created to answer the evaluator's most important question: "Why should we select you?" and is repeated in subtle ways throughout the entry. Creating a win theme has several benefits – it can help organise your entry strategy, it grabs the judges' attention and differentiates your submission, giving the evaluators great reasons to select you.

When scripting your response, cross-reference the themes, but don't constantly refer to text in the other sections of the entry. A judge will have read the original question several times, and they won't want to keep checking back and forth through the submission. Making the flow disjointed may mean that they lose their place in the story you are delivering about your achievements.

When asked what elements you should avoid in your award entry, Caroline, Gaby and Roni provided the following insight.

Caroline and Gaby:

> Try to keep it very focused, use bullet points rather than longer worded paragraphs.

Roni:

> Make it genuine, write from your heart and be honest. I don't have a structure. I am very passionate about what I do, but I am also very committed to helping others as well. So I just tell them the truth. Just be honest about what you have done and what you have achieved.

What Extra Supporting Documents Should I Include?

Again, you will need to read the exact award requirements in the entry process.

You should expect to include:

- Your business plan

- Proof of your accounts and trading success

- Details of your marketing plan and examples of marketing materials

Then develop the *wow* factor – what is going to make you stand out?

This might include:

- Testimonials and case studies from your delighted clients

  o These can be made as graphics or videos if you really want to wow the judges

  o Ensure each named person is accredited

- Statistics from your customers showing the impact you have delivered (including satisfaction surveys)

- Statements from staff and your business supporters

- Information on internships, training and customer care

- Photos of major events you have delivered, such as speaking engagements

- Details of social value and community engagement projects you have supported

- Scans of PR coverage

- Highlight professional accreditations, such as your continuing professional development, memberships and qualifications relevant to your application

- Share a link to a video and host it on YouTube or your website

- Feature your reviews on Facebook or Google, or industry specific review sites, as these provide great independent validation

- Create cartoons and infographics – illustrate your entry to make your entry stand out

We recommend that you support your application with facts about your business and showcase your achievements with clear evidence. Remember to tell your story – the judges want to hear about your individual business journey, your challenges and your triumphs. Make sure this is put across with passion, and that your format is easy and interesting to read. You need facts and figures, so forget the fluffy, vague comments – they won't cut it!

Writing the Award

Make your entry stand out:

- Colours

- Imagery

- Short and easy to read paragraphs

- Headings and sub-headings

- Graphs and tables

Keep your writing simple:

- No jargon or unexplained acronyms

- Don't create difficult to digest sentences or huge chunks of text

- Use facts, figures, bullet points

Cross reference themes between questions:

- But don't say 'as stated in question X'

- The marker may not have had the whole entry to assess

Insights from Award Entrant, Judge and Organiser – Tony Robinson OBE

Tony Robinson OBE is the Micro Business Champion and co-founder of #MicroBizMattersDay, an annual global day of live streaming of business owners' tips and insights. Tony is focused on helping to "make business life better for micro enterprise owners".

The idea for this book is great and made me realise what an important part of my professional life, and life as a business owner, awards have been. I've founded and hosted five national awards programmes and events, judged over 50 and been invited as a guest or speaker at over 200 awards ceremonies. So, you can tell I'm a fan of awards and the benefits they can bring to the entrants.

Winning is great, but it's still a brilliant boost to your career and business to be shortlisted, and to attend the awards event. The benefits are not just PR and making your team, customers and suppliers, proud to be working with you. Awards programmes can raise the standards and the pursuit of excellence in whole sectors, vocations, regions, cities and towns.

Being associated with excellence and gaining an award from your peers puts you in the spotlight for career and business opportunities at the highest level. This is why awards programmes and events are so important to building a trusted brand – even if the brand is just you. For example, when I founded the SFEDI Group in 1996 to improve the skills of startup and existing business owners in the UK, and all those that support them, we developed an awards programme and major annual event to showcase the best in each sector from government, to the media, influential entrepreneurs and the entire business support community.

Our first event was at the Bank of England, and I know that kick-started many business owners and business support personnel to new opportunities. The awards are still running annually, now at the House of Lords, and many of the entrants and winners say they've made contacts at the awards events that have taken them to a new level. Indeed, the chair of SFEDI Group and the Institute of Enterprise and Entrepreneurs, Ruth Lowbridge MBE, was one of the early winners whom we invited on to the board. Many winners became suppliers to organisations I was associated with and some of our sponsors, including government.

My hero and inspiration for many of the subsequent awards programmes I've developed, such as the #MicroBizMatters Day, and Movement, which I co-founded, is Kanya King CBE, who is founder of the MOBO Awards. The MOBO Awards have created and promoted new talent. It is now among many of the world's greatest names in urban music and has exported British urban music acts around the world. If you ever find your career or business flatlining, one of the fastest ways to get yourself into the mindset of the influencers in your sector is to win or be shortlisted for an award.

Awards have been incredibly important for the business I've founded and run over the last 30 years. Our very first award was local, from Milton Keynes Chamber of Commerce, and led to our first government contract – pretty important as government spend is hundreds of billions of pounds. Last year the Enterprise Agency I chair won a prestigious national award from our sector body and that really completed our rebranding and has made our CEO one of the most influential in the sector.

My favourite personal award was at the House of Commons in 2012, from the International Association of Bookkeepers.

It was a Lifetime Achievement Award for Entrepreneurship. I received two such Lifetime Achievement Awards that year – I'm not sure if they thought I was going to snuff it – anyway, I'm still here and still championing micro business owners everywhere.

More recently I submitted a testimony for a LinkedIn Leadership Award. I explained why Tina Boden, my co-founder of #MicroBizMatters Day and Movement should win this award. We didn't win, but LinkedIn is very influential and there were an incredible number of entries – thousands. We got into the final 10 and were invited to a posh reception, with many amazing leaders. We also got to meet Sir Alex Ferguson at the Royal Festival Hall before attending a major event to launch his new book on leadership. Well worth the entry.

There have been many inspiring and emotional moments, and many winners of awards are now colleagues and collaborators. As judges, we don't know about personal circumstances, illnesses, disabilities and sometimes tragic events. It is always uplifting for everyone in the room to know the joy that deserved recognition through an award can come.

My funniest moment was in retrospect – it didn't feel funny at the time. In 2007 my business partner Clare, and an events organiser, Justine, who was a previous award winner, put together at very short notice a SFEDI Awards event on HMS Belfast. It was short notice because it was something of a relaunch after a difficult time on funding and government policy. I'm not the most organised person in the world, and I was scared stiff that very few people, including the award winners, would come. I just spread the word and asked others to spread the word.

> Double the number of people we had catered for arrived – we nearly sank HMS Belfast. Among the mayhem of not enough chairs or food or drink, I had to feverishly look among the large crowd to see if any of the award winners were present before announcing that award. Mayhem, but it was a massive success and is still talked about decades later.

Thanks for sharing Tony.

Busting the Myths Around Award Entry by Gavan Wall

Gavan Wall is a multi-award-winning businessman who, with his business The Wall Group, has won a variety of different awards. These include the Digital Business Person of the Year at the DANI Awards, Community Business of the Year, a Store Award, Business of the Year and he was part of Belfast's Best Top 50 Entrepreneurs.

As well as running The Wall Group, Gavan hosts *The Speed Mentor* podcast, which covers different business-related topics to help people succeed. After changing from a legal background to a career in business, he recognised the benefits of winning awards and recommends all businesses apply for them.

We spoke to Gavan and he identified and resolved some of the myths that are associated with business awards. He then addressed the reasons why people *should* be applying:

> 1. 'They're a fix. They're all a fix.' Now, maybe they are a fix, and maybe they aren't. Maybe you're not in the right clique, maybe you are. Sometimes you will get the benefit of the judges' preferences and other times it will go against you. So, get into one or two of the

cliques. You'll win and you'll lose. Sometimes it might be unfair, sometimes it might not be, but just keep pushing.

2. 'It's not worth the hassle.' There are so many benefits to award winning, which I hope I will highlight to you.

3. 'It's only for show offs.' Never mind the show offs. This is your chance to showcase yourself.

4. 'I don't have the time.' Put award ceremonies in your marketing campaign, or your budget, and make the time and money available.

5. 'What if I don't win?' But what if you do win?

6. 'It's just a big drinking session.' It's only a boozy session if you make it one. I don't drink and I get huge value from these events specifically because I don't drink, and I'm able to extract the marrow from the bone of these events. I listen intently to industry peers and rivals and I make the most of the opportunity to listen to what they're talking about. I get all the inside secret sauce. It's strategic, and it works. So, don't be drinking (too much) at these events.

7. 'They're a money-making racket for the organisers.' Why would you worry if they're a money-making racket for the organisers, or not? What are you worried about? Who cares if other people make money? This is all about you showcasing yourself and *you* making money.

8. 'They take up too much time.' If this is an issue, you need to leverage and outsource to make more time to work on your business rather than just in it.

Don't be thinking small, don't be thinking small-minded, small horizons, small attitudes, small company. Because if awards aren't on your agenda, that's when you'll end up being small in your life. The benefits of participating in, never mind winning, business awards are immeasurable.

Now here are all the reasons why you should get involved:

1. Take advantage of the marketing opportunity. Whether you're making a speech at an event, or being a finalist at an awards event, there's nothing quite like it to develop and improve your personal brand awareness. Now remember, it's not just about the people in the room. Social media will be covered in pictures and posts about the event. Other people will be helping market your business. They'll be taking pictures and putting them on their social media. Not to mention local or national press might be there to give you an opportunity. Somebody else will take a picture of you potentially winning an award or being highly commended and post that on their timeline. That's very valuable.

2. Recognition has two elements to it. For you it's a thumbs up from your peers that you're getting somewhere, and for your team it's to show them that you're interested enough, and thankful enough, that they've made such great efforts that you take the time to get your business involved in these events.

3. Use the opportunity to spread the message. You could send out a thank you to everybody you're doing business with to thank them for helping you during the year you won the award. How powerful would that be? So, you're winning an award and you're not just revelling

in the award, you're sending out a thank you note to your suppliers, you're sending out a thank you note to your customers, you're sending out a thank you note to your bank saying "thanks so much for supporting us this year and look, we've just won an award because of your support" that's powerful stuff.

4. You've set yourself apart from the competition. You've been better or different or certainly cared a little bit more about your business, and you've been able to celebrate that.

5. You can use the achievement of the award ceremonies. Build it into your marketing plan and wear your accolade with pride.

6. What will your customers think? Sometimes the decision between going with one business, as a customer, and going with another, is decided by very fine margins. Now make sure that when the decision is being made the client is factoring in that your business is an award-winning business.

7. What sort of effect will it have on the morale? Maybe you'll take the whole team to the event and make an incredible experience out of it. Your team will be proud.

8. Award winning will help you to recruit. The best people in your industry will want to work for the best business in the industry.

9. Winners will want to cosy up, share ideas and share opportunities with you as another winner.

10. Get on your LinkedIn and other social media channels and use your moment in the sun to reach out to other businesses that you could build up partnerships with or form alliances with.

11. This one is hugely important. You and your team now hold yourself to a higher standard as there's now a level of service, of expectation, of standard that you've achieved and that you've evidenced to the world. When you're tempted to take shortcuts in the future, this level of expectation will help keep you and your team at that higher level. That's hugely important for your future success. So, you've reached that higher level, you've reached that new standard, your own team expects it of you, you expect it of yourself, your customer expect it of you, your business partners expect it of themselves and now you're operating at a whole new level. Your business can take off.

I know it's a cliché but, if you're not in, you can't win. If you're pushing away free marketing opportunities like these, you're missing out. Don't kid yourself otherwise. Get involved, think about the win, and don't let the naysayers affect your mindset about how important awards are.

Thanks for your insight Gavan.

Understanding The Judges' Needs

Judges are human beings and they will make judgments. They really don't want a wall of text with spelling and grammar errors throughout. An entry full of errors and typos does not represent the best version of your business. It may create the impression of a lack of attention to detail, or carelessness – things you don't want associated with your company.

You will need to edit and proofread your entry, preferably more than once. You really need to go through this process of making sure your entry is the optimal version of the professionalism you want to reflect.

The submission needs to provide an honest representation of your business – support this with facts and figures that are relevant to the response, and add in your client testimonials. You can make these more eye-catching by changing the format, so they could be shown as graphics or as a standout piece of text with quote marks, depending on the format of the submission.

It is important that you support any claims you make with hard facts, figures and proof, and you must include a significant number of facts and figures throughout every answer. Rather than saying: "We have grown significantly in the last year." Say: "Our turnover has doubled in this past year from X to Y, and we have employed X number of new employees." The evidence is key to winning – the judge wants to know what sets you apart from any other business, and so it is vital that you provide solid evidence. Anybody can say that their business has grown, it is the figures that become a measurable way of evaluating your success.

Always be honest with your entry. Don't lie, make up figures or avoid mentioning something that the general business community will know about you. If you have had a challenging year, say so. Follow that up with why it was a challenge, what you learned and explain how you are going to increase your efforts or refocus the next time. Being sincere and explaining your challenges is very powerful as it shows you are constantly learning.

The judges for your awards are usually experienced business owners, investors and experts in their fields. This means that they are experienced enough to see through any attempt to cover up your weaknesses. If you feel as if you need to lie to get noticed or be considered in a category – don't enter. You need to choose categories to enter based on your, and your business's true strengths. If there are weaknesses, don't cover them up. If they are not relevant, then there is no explicit need to mention them. However, any weaknesses relevant to your application should be declared, and explained.

For example, you may have made a trading loss in the previous year because of significant investment that should pay off in the following years. Don't gloss over the fact that you have made a loss – explain why this was the case, what investment you have made and how you expect this will pay dividends in the future. If you have invested £10,000 in some new machinery that will allow you to make more products in the following year that will in turn increase your profits in the future, there is no harm in declaring this loss. Rather, what would harm your application is to ignore your loss by avoiding declaring your profits for a particular year – this would immediately tell a judge that you are hiding something.

Judges will almost certainly assess the data at Companies House and are likely to be financially savvy themselves. Many judging panels have an accountant as part of the assessment team, as it is such an important element of the entry.

We feature specific insight from two award judges: Anita Jaynes, who runs the Techie Awards, and Alec Jones-Hall, who runs the South West Business and Community Awards. Their useful feedback can be seen later in the book.

Remember to describe what you do in straightforward terms. When you are on the inside of a business it can sometimes prove difficult to explain what you do in an easy to understand way. When you know your business, you have the tendency to explain in granular detail, as you want to portray the complexity of the everyday life of the company. Instead, explain what your business does in a manner you would tell a seven-year-old. You want the definition to be totally self-explanatory, so it allows someone to know exactly what you do without superfluous detail.

You will see the question: "Explain in simple terms what your business does" featured in almost every set of award questions for any category. It is critical that you use this opportunity to explain exactly what your business is and how it works in the most simple and easy to understand way possible. It is more than likely that the judge has never heard of your business, especially if you are a startup or a small business.

Making your business model clear for the judges creates a solid basis for their understanding of the merits and standout USPs of your business. Judges want to be able to see how a business makes money, where the profit is derived from and how it is sustainable. They don't want to spend time working out how your business model actually works as a credible company. Don't make it difficult for them to make a judgment on the success of your business.

Make It Simple for the Judges

Your proofing process should also consider the following: Who are the judges? What audience are you trying to impress? You may have quite a mixture of personalities that will be looking for different things in your entry. It is often the case that an entry will be judged by several people, after which they will consolidate their feedback before agreeing on the final result. Among these personality types could be a technical expert who might know your field in a good level of detail, or a procurement professional who might be looking for something different because they are used to judging as a purchaser.

You may find that sponsors are also involved in assessment, and their agenda may be completely different. Of course, you may have a celebrity or a big name to add kudos or a PR boost to the process. There is always the chance that they will be anonymous, in which case, all you can do is put your best case forward but recognise there will be no chance of developing a relationship.

We recommend that you understand who the judging panel is (if this is possible). If you understand what they are interested in and what drives them, you can weave the relevant themes into your entry. If you know their details (for example, they are featured on the awards website), you might want to send them a LinkedIn request to connect in advance, so you build a bit of a relationship with them. It will not usually affect the outcome of any judging process, but if you are connected on social media, they will start to see all the content you are sharing and this will build a broader picture of what you deliver as a business, your interests and how you interact with your network.

Certainly, if you have been notified as a finalist, you might want to connect with them to say how delighted you are to be a finalist, and how much you are looking forward to meeting them at the awards ceremony. It's all part of that engagement process – showcasing that you understand their expectations of those who enter and how this is matched and reflected in your entry. Make sure that your social media profile backs up the story you have presented. Let them see what you did, how it made a difference, and what the output was. Structure your response with a beginning, middle and end, reflecting the great storytelling tradition. Exhibit the logic that the judges can easily follow, supported with a narrative that allows them to see what you went through along the way. Ongoing engagement is a continuing chapter in the assessment journey.

Debbie:

> If it's a postal entry, present your content in a nice folder or have it bound, make it clear and easy to read. Remember to make it look like a business presentation.

Present the document as it has been requested. If the rules request that the entry should be provided in a given format, for example a Word or PDF file format, then provide it that way. This also means keeping to the prescribed structure and question order – please don't respond to the questions in the wrong order, this only makes the assessor's job more of a challenge, and you run the real risk of annoying them. Not only is it more difficult to compare against the other submissions that you are being marked against, but you have made it harder psychologically for them to award you credit.

If you have been presented with a question that has four specific elements, answer those four aspects in the required order. If you are allowed, add additional supporting information, such as examples of press coverage, or images – then make sure you reference them. The rules will state whether you are allowed attachments or not, but the judge will need to understand their relevance and link them with the main entry to get the full picture.

During the assessment process, the judges may request further information from you. If this is required, make sure you respond promptly. This is a strong signal that they are showing interest in your entry and they need more detail to clarify their understanding.

You may also get the opportunity to provide up-to-date information, particularly if there has been a large time window between submission and assessment. For example, the award organisers may provide the opportunity to supply any new case studies or updated financial information. If this is requested, then always take this as a good opportunity to provide more data to support your award entry.

Make Sure You Include Everything That Is Requested of You

As already mentioned, you need to ensure you have answered every question, but you also need to make sure that you have attached any extra information they request. It is not unusual for awards to ask or allow you to attach supporting documents, whether that is financial information, business plans, testimonials, images, copies of press coverage, customer quotes, TripAdvisor reviews or videos that paint your business in a good light. Not including these is as detrimental to your application as not answering the questions. Make sure your supporting information looks good and is in the right format.

> Make it succinct, get your point across and respect the time it takes for judges to read your entries. Don't just aim to fill up the space and don't repeat yourself. If you need help, get others to assist you who can polish your entry and make sure it reads well.

What Are The Judges Looking For?

Judges will be looking for evidence to back up your claims. They will want to see how your business leads the industry, and the methods that you employ to innovate. Judges will require the entrant to validate their story and prove the benefits that were delivered. They are often really interested in the challenges faced. Don't be afraid to include something that went badly but do identify how you overcame it.

Of real interest is your unique business story. Why did you start? Did you need a lifestyle change or was change thrust upon you? Was there a gap in the market that you identified when you needed a product or service yourself that was not provided? How did you develop your brand? Who helped you get your journey underway? What have been the hardest aspects... and the most enjoyable ones?

The judges are keen to understand the challenges that you have overcome as a business, as these prove your resilience, determination and drive for success even in tough times. All of these attributes will be looked for as evidence. It is not just the issues that you faced, but the methods you have employed to overcome them and what you have learned that will make your business stronger for the future.

Judges don't just want to read about how you reacted to market conditions, they want to really understand how you changed or challenged an evolving market. Be creative. To win, your application needs to stand out from the rest, so make your business come alive to the judges.

Tell them what opportunity you saw but explain why it was a good challenge and what you did to shape it to your advantage. Show how you were dynamic, as that will give you the standout required to win an award. Demonstrate how you shaped events rather than purely reacted to them. Demonstrate how you anticipated problems and what mediation measures you enacted. Did you see that your client had identified a specific issue, and you realised that this may be common for all your clients and therefore changed your business process? What benefit did this ultimately deliver? Explain in detail.

Provide your examples in the context of your business activity, so the judges can understand the nature of the challenge, the predicted problem, the solution and the named benefit. They want to understand how you created a successful outcome that embraced the change and how you built upon it.

Sustainability and Corporate Social Responsibility (CSR) usually feature highly in award entry criteria. You will need to understand these key elements so you can leverage the impact they have made within your business during the award application writing process.

CSR refers to how a company operates in a socially and environmentally responsible manner when dealing with key stakeholders. While CSR is most often related to large corporations, small businesses also benefit from socially responsible practices. CSR activity can range from waste and pollution reduction, to employee volunteering hours, it also encompasses support of charities and funding for community projects.

During the judging process, you will need to show the demonstrable benefit of your CSR efforts and these need to focus both on what you did and why it was significant to your business. The assessment will consider how the activity was important to your staff, your stakeholders, and the broader community, so you need to be able to explain this. You might choose to do good because it makes you feel good, but CSR is an important indicator of company culture and a driver for future staff wanting to work for you. Demonstrating commitment to a strong community ethos is also a positive selection criterion for clients, as it is known to additionally have a good effect on your bottom line. There is a lot of data now proving that socially responsible companies are more profitable than those that are not.

Successful businesses are now expected to give something back, but there is a recognition of what is possible relative to the scale of your business. It is certainly about sharing wealth and sharing opportunity. If you can't give cash, you can give time or you can give expertise. This may be as simple as helping at a local school to assist in their curriculum, or mock interviews. You could also provide people with opportunities, which might include apprenticeships, internships or work experience.

> Have you got a company charity? This is a great focus for fundraising, and you can allow your staff to nominate their favourite charities on to a shortlist and even hold a vote on which charity you will select. Some organisations support a charity on an ongoing basis, and others change their charity so there is a charity of the year. Purpol have a company charity that is our focus, which means we can see

the difference our contribution makes over a period of time. Make sure you include your charitable support on the entry and include the logo as well for additional impact.

Judges really do look for how you are nurturing your employees, and they like to see proof of elements such as employee welfare, particularly for training and development initiatives. Does your company have a corporate charity? Do you provide the opportunity to volunteer or provide sponsorship for the local school's sports kit? Did you hold a charity cake bake, or provide work experience for local students? Take photos of these activities where appropriate and evidence your CSR support in your entry.

Insight From the Judges

We now hear from two award judges, Alec Jones-Hall, who founded Great British Expos and the Thames Valley/South West Business and Community Awards; and Anita Jaynes, founder of the Business Exchange magazines and The Techies – an award scheme that specifically recognises those in the technology sector.

Can you explain the typical judging process?

Alec Jones-Hall:

Basically, we have the nominations come in to us. First, we look at how detailed they are, so we want to have a look at whether someone has submitted their company accounts, their company profitability and testimonials, as they are key. We also want to understand the company history and how that company has developed and what their aspirations are. So, we go through that process and if a nomination hasn't got that in, then they won't be shortlisted. You can't make an informed decision if you haven't got historic data. How can you decide that somebody's worthy of an award when they may have terrible historic data?

Anita Jaynes:

> So for our awards, 'The Techies', we have a process where
> people apply, and the entries come through to us. Entrants
> are asked if they want to supply supporting material, so
> if they want to, they can provide a video plus images that
> validate an entry. When that information comes through to
> us, we submit it to all of our judges to read, and choose
> their favourites. We then all get around a table and have a
> discussion about the ones that they the judges have selected
> and they will then score them. Usually, the points score
> determines the winners straight away, unless there is some
> additional information that needs to be assessed.

What do you look for in a winning entry?

Alec Jones-Hall:

> It's got to be the fact that they have strong customer
> testimonials, they have good accounts and good profitability
> within the business. If it's a business award then they must
> be profitable, have company growth year on year, and they
> must be very forward thinking and show how they are going
> to be innovating and on future trend.

Anita Jaynes:

> The key thing when entering any award scheme is to answer
> the questions. I think people tie themselves up in knots, be
> clear and concise. A short entry can be the winning entry. It
> doesn't need to be really long, it's about getting your message
> across clearly about who you are, what you do, answering the
> question and providing stats to validate and substantiate. For
> example, you can't say you're a world leader unless you've
> got something to prove you're a world leader.

What are the most common errors in the entries that you see?

Alec Jones-Hall:

Lack of detail, lack of content. People don't give details of their accounts, customer testimonials or even what their vision is for their company. How can judges be excited about your company and want to reward you if they haven't got the detail? How can they think this is a worthy candidate if you haven't been shouting about what you have done? When it comes to judging, there are so many nominations to read through that a judge will skim read. We do check Companies House, and we check people's websites and look at whether they have testimonials – so we do a lot of background checks. We also Google the company in the news section, so we can see if they have press releases and what they are doing for the community. When we get nominations in, we need to verify the detail that's been put on the actual nomination form.

Anita Jaynes:

Not answering the question. If you have the opportunity to upload a video about your business, to supply images and background information, then make sure you supply it because this info can really showcase your business. If you've got the opportunity to do it then flaunt it and make sure that if you are driving someone to a page on your website that it's got all the key information about you. Make sure that everything is there, with no mistakes, and that the page hasn't suddenly gone down. It's your shop window and you need to ensure that you make the most of the opportunity.

What makes an entry stand out for you?

Alec Jones-Hall:

Again, it would be the accounts, the profitability, the growth of the business and how they treat their staff. If they are an equal opportunities employer, and whether or not they have made investment in their employees. Also, what their aspirations are for the business, and what awards they have won previously.

Anita Jaynes:

Entries that are concise and get to the crux of it straight away with key stats. Bullet pointed information with punchy headlines that grab your attention. Make sure you detail all of your achievements relevant to the award you are applying for.

Comment on the worst entry you have seen.

Alec Jones-Hall:

I had one entry where the entrant stated they should win the award because they were a really nice person.

Anita Jaynes:

The worst entries are the lazy ones. We get lots of them and they just include words for words' sake, without thinking about why they are writing them or what value it adds to the application. You really need to think about your answers and make time to apply properly. Don't submit an entry on a Friday afternoon with half an hour to spare. Spend time thinking about your entry. Look at who entered last year, read any judges' comments on what made the winning entry stand out and use this information to your advantage. What makes you different? Can you include client testimonials?

Project results? My biggest tip would be, if you're entering an award for a particular project you've completed, make sure that you tailor-make your submission. So many companies submit generic information about their business when they should be being very specific about how they have contributed or made a difference through their work.

Why do you enjoy being a judge?

Alec Jones-Hall:

We enjoy rewarding business. We know how hard it is to be an entrepreneur. Sometimes I think it can be a very lonely place, trying to plug your business, trying to win business and sometimes your family don't understand. I think going to an award ceremony of your peers, where you're being celebrated and rewarded, can be wonderful. Also, we have got so many success stories of businesses that have won the award that have then gone on to win tenders, get new business, new funding and speaking opportunities. They actually have an accolade that can be life-changing to some businesses.

Anita Jaynes:

I love discovering businesses that I didn't know existed before the awards. There are so many amazing companies that fall under the radar because they are just busy doing what they do. Being a judge really opens your eyes to the diversity of a business landscape, showcasing and putting the spotlight on firms you wouldn't know about. I also enjoy spending time with the other judges and getting to know them. I've met some really inspiring people when volunteering my time as a judge, that have made a real impact on me and how I want to be perceived as a business person and entrepreneur.

What is the worst behaviour you have seen at an awards ceremony?

Alec Jones-Hall:

I have seen people get absolutely legless, seeing it as a 'jolly'. They have been really disrespectful. The thing is, you are representing your business at that awards ceremony, and you're in a room with all your peers, media, sponsors and corporates. So, if you are going to be getting the accolade, you have got to represent yourself as if you are worthy of it. I have had people asking for the judges' comments and asking why they haven't won, and then people doing press releases or going on social media because they haven't won. I think, be grateful and apply again next year, and be thankful that you have been shortlisted. I think it's good to get feedback when you're given it and to take it on board.

Anita Jaynes:

Businesses assuming that they would win or thinking that they had won. It's just poor form and comes across as arrogant! Be graceful whether winning or losing.

As a judge I am always keen to submit notes on why I've chosen an entrant as my winner and why I've not selected others. Then, if a company or individual asks for feedback post award ceremony, it can be delivered in a constructive way. Being a poor loser doesn't do anything for anyone. There is no point in entering awards if you know you can't handle losing. It's not good for your business. Remember, you're doing this to leave a good impression of your business – whether you win or lose!

What has been the most magical moment at an awards ceremony?

Alec Jones-Hall:

> It is so lovely to see people who perhaps weren't expecting to win, and they have actually won. That's the most magical moment. Just seeing how people and entrepreneurs made such great sacrifices to run successful businesses then suddenly seeing that sacrifice being awarded and thinking wow, I am starting to be recognised for all the late nights and 60-hour weeks.

Anita Jaynes:

> It was magical to see our 'Future Tech Superstar' take to the stage to collect his award at this year's Techies. He was so surprised to win, was incredibly nervous on stage, but managed to get his words out and delivered a really endearing and inspiring speech. I'm hoping it gave him the confidence to fly even further in his career.

Amazing insight from Anita and Alec on what you should consider for a judge-friendly entry.

Maximise Your Chances Of Winning

The million pound question – how do you maximise your chances of winning? First off, you need to showcase your strategic thinking. Most business awards want to know how you excel in the world of business, so you will need to practically demonstrate the application of your strategic thinking and the processes that are followed for decision making. Establish proof to show how you have adapted to events. It might be you have had to respond to a factor totally outside your control, such as a new piece of legislation that has been enacted and has a major impact on your company. There is always a positive in displaying how your business has been impacted by change as it provides the opportunity to show how the firm has adapted, and that's a great story to tell.

Second, think about your financials. Usually you need to show a core level of growth. Now that might not be an overall turnover growth, but it might be that you divested in one given business area and concentrated on another, or that you have reduced turnover to focus on profitability. The judges will be looking for a sustainable business with a track record of ongoing success. Client retention is another factor that is often considered, as returning clients are a great indicator of a successful business that is servicing its customers well. You might like to highlight that retained clients contribute X per cent of turnover and X per cent of profitability.

It is likely, as part of the assessment, that the judges will be doing financial stress testing on your accounts. They will also be looking at where you have been, where you are coming from and potentially where you are going in monetary terms. Ensure you know those financial criteria but also consider other success measures such as customer service feedback questionnaires, proportion of returning customers, and uplift in the value of spend for key clients.

Examples of innovation and improvement are another one of the areas that any person writing an award entry sometimes struggles with. Often this stems from the difficulty in understanding what is meant by innovation. What one person thinks is innovative, another may think is standard working practice, so it is often worthwhile clarifying what is perceived as innovation for that specific award.

Many businesses are innovating constantly, and as this is their 'business as usual' it is unlikely that every innovation always gets documented thoroughly. It is useful to capture a diary of innovation as and when it occurs. Within most small businesses, asking what you did a month ago is often hard to remember. Capturing information as you go, even catching things you have done each month, will ease the burden and help provide evidence and a prompt when you need it.

When you are composing your entry, make the most of the word or page count limits. They provide a direct indication of the level of detail that judges want and expect to see. If you have been asked for a 10-page response, then that is what they expect to see. Most entries do not require a vast response, as what they really want you to do is be succinct, impactful and to wow them. Make sure you keep the content relevant and always link back to the benefits delivered for your client. This is where testimonials and endorsements are so powerful, a third-party confirmation of what you are stating adds real weight to your response.

Lastly, start early. Developing responses can take a long time. When you are running a business, you want the end result of an award but probably not the actual process of the entry. It is the quality of the entry that will determine success, and remember they can only judge you on what you put down on the form, not what they already know about your business. Despite the long process, entering does have value as it allows you to assess the current state of your business.

Unfortunately, there is no quick and easy way to write a good entry – it takes time, effort and patience. So, start early and try to give yourself at least a month to gather all the data you will need and leave enough time to write and edit your entry.

If you are targeting an award, do your homework in the first year and develop that structure to identify what is wanted by the judges. When you have had the opportunity to get to know the awards judging process a bit better, and you have had a dialogue with people who have won, you'll be able to find out what they did, and you can learn from it. This means you can then incorporate that information into your awards process the next time around for a greater chance of future success.

> While we have been lucky enough to win some awards at the first attempt, we attest to the value of perseverance and have won three national awards at the second attempt, including the Great British Entrepreneur of the Year Awards (GBEA), the Best Business Women Awards and the Women in Marketing Awards. Even if you are entering again for a different category, building a relationship with the award

brand and personnel will allow greater understanding of the process and put you in a better position to win next time.

Understanding which awards can have greatest impact for your business is key to both selecting the awards to target and maximising your chance of winning.

Roni, when asked which awards have had the greatest impact on her business, commented:

> Every single award I win is a pleasant surprise. There are always so many deserving people in the room. As a result, each award means something slightly different. Each award is special. I must say that it was great to be awarded Black British Business Person of the Year 2018, sponsored by Bloomberg, in a room full of leaders of large corporates, where I picked up the award of the night for a company I founded myself. It was a similar feeling being named Best Consultant and Distinguished Winner at the WICE awards. They were extremely emotional moments. When I won the NatWest Awards, it was possibly the most nerve-wracking, as both my parents were with me.

Caroline also acknowledged the importance of targeting key awards but also their associated benefits:

> I have been to award ceremonies alone, which is always daunting, but at one I actually ended up sitting next to a person from an IT company who told me about the Goldman Sachs 10,000 Small Business programme. Because of that, we applied and successfully went through the programme. On the other side of me was someone who then introduced Turtle Tots to a company that were potential investors. In terms of credibility, I think winning an award three years running gave us a lot of standing and great name recognition.

The Importance of Proofreading

We always say you should avoid proofreading your own content. Sometimes this is not easily achievable if you are the only person in your business, but it is a valuable exercise to get a second pair of eyes to review your entry submission. If it is not possible, many programs, including Word, have a read aloud feature which can be beneficial as it lets you hear what is written down, as opposed to seeing what you want to be there.

Once you have written the initial award entry, it is vital you spend time perfecting it. Allocate time to complete several drafts of your entry, as the first one is likely to need improving. Make sure every response answers the question asked and that the writing flows well. Not only does it need to make sense, but the claims made need to be backed up by facts and figures.

Proofreading is hard – the brain plays tricks on you by looking for shortcuts, so you often become blind to your own errors. This is why we state the importance of an independent review. We appreciate this might feel against your better instincts, because you have crafted a beautiful entry, and inviting someone to tear it apart is not the thing you feel best inclined to do. However, you want someone to check the logic and flow as well as the content. Treat the reviewing and proofing process like an internal assessment, provide the reviewer with the question you were asked as well as the marking scheme. Let them examine the response and confirm that it matches the requirements.

Getting a third party to read your application and provide some constructive feedback will improve your entry by confirming it matches the criteria of the award category and whether the spelling and grammar is correct. However, don't just rely on someone else to check your entry. Leave yourself enough time to take a couple of days break from your work as this will help you gain a fresh perspective and make it easier to check for coherence, grammar, typos and spelling mistakes. It can also help to print out your entry – reading an entry in printed form can help make it easier to see any issues. Reach out to your social media connections as they may well volunteer to help.

By the end of this process, you will likely have spent hours working on your award and just want to be rid of it. Try to avoid the urge to send it off without reading it over a few times yourself. This is one of the last stages. Imagine that you have narrowly missed the top spot – what could you have done better? What do you think might have got you a few extra marks? What would you have changed if you could write the whole thing again? You might be surprised at how effective and worthwhile a bit of self-critiquing can be in affecting the quality of your submission. If you have found improvements that could be made, take the time to make the changes as the effort will pay off in the end. Proofread for spelling and grammatical mistakes once more and then your entry should be ready for submission.

If you are going to ask someone to proofread, give them enough time. You are asking them to give you feedback, but most importantly for you, there needs to be enough time for you to edit your response, having taken that feedback on board. You will be wasting everybody's time if you ask for an assessment and then don't do anything with the findings. Build this edit phase into your process timeline.

As well as compelling content, you need to get the basics right – applications with typos, confusing formatting and impenetrable jargon make it very difficult to succeed in awards.

Debbie offers the following summary:

> Make sure you check and double check the spellings and grammar and select an easy to read font. Use bullet points rather than write long paragraphs to make it easier for the judges and remember to stick to any word count.

What to Do If You Don't Get to the Finals

It's the shortlist publication day... what do you do when you get the results via email, or they are uploaded on the website, and after checking several times for your name, the realisation dawns that you have not made it through to the finalist selection?

OUCH.

It hurts, but you must move on.

Debbie Gilbert summarised the reasons why entries can fail to make the finalist list:

Awards are a business competition, and therefore not everyone is shortlisted. Often entries do not get shortlisted because there is missing information crucial to the judging process.

Below are the reasons Debbie provides for why entries do not make the final cut:

- Lack of evidence

- Did not answer the question asked

- Incomplete information

- Repeated response in more than one question

- Wrong category entered

- Did not match eligibility criteria

- Business passion and story not communicated

- Even trying to enter multiple times with separate entries

Assess what you included against the criteria and be honest. Take what you have learned and use it for a future award entry. We cover the recovery phase later in the 'What To Do If You Don't Win' section.

Attending the Awards

Should I go? Is it worth the money? Should I take someone with me? These are some of the questions you might have once you have submitted the award entry and have been shortlisted or made it as a finalist. Attending the award ceremony itself can be expensive, but you have made it to the final – so it is time to celebrate, invite your team and book your ticket.

If you need to watch the budget, you can cut down on costs by just attending on your own, especially if you are a small business. The more awards you go to, the more you will realise that only the bigger businesses will book out an entire table or more – many business owners will go alone or will send one representative from their company, and you will be seated with a selection of other people who are not in big parties. You will not be isolated, and this also creates the perfect opportunity to network and get to know others in your industry or locality.

Some award structures may only award the winner if they are there on the night to receive their prize, however, the ceremony needs to be thought of as a chance to make maximum use of the publicity opportunities available to you as a finalist. Taking photos on the night (or rarely in the day) and live tweeting or uploading to your social media accounts during and after the event is an important way to engage with the awards structure and gain some meaningful traction on social media.

If you are shortlisted, you may have media opportunities presented – such as radio interviews or the chance to feature in a blog. Seize these occasions as they are great ways to promote your business regardless of the outcome of the next stage. In truth, most of the audience will never hear about the eventual outcome anyway, so the win is in the very opportunity that you have just exploited.

Never forget the award ceremony is the chance to promote your business, and in our case, we use it to reflect the colour purple in our brand and company name. Having an extensive collection of purple dresses for all occasions means that if there is ever a photo opportunity, the Purpol Marketing 'purpleness' is reinforced. If you have a brand colour, take the opportunity to build this into your awards attire – it gives an additional chance for connection and another reason to talk about your business.

If you can't be there, don't be afraid to be there socially instead. There was an award ceremony where I was a finalist and could not attend due to a bid writing deadline. I sent my apologies and retweeted the event and shared posts all evening instead.

What to Do If You Don't Win

You are at the awards ceremony having been named as a finalist, you have navigated the three courses of the meal, been careful not to spill dinner down your finest attire, and not dared to drink too much. The programme is positioned on the table, and you have read it at least three times, trying to remember the order of the award announcements.

The compere starts to read out the attributes of the winning company, and your heart is thumping in your chest as the evidence is emerging that it's not you. Following that, they call another entrepreneur or business name, and they (and not you) get to take the walk of fame up to the stage to collect their trophy and champagne, to the adulation of the crowd.

ARGGHHHHH.

You are no doubt using your best poker face, clapping for the winner and taking commiserations from your friends at the table.

Losing out on the top prize should not be thought of as defeat. If you are shortlisted or end up as a finalist but fail to win the overall category, it is important not to be deflated.

All award entrants will go through this and the more awards you enter the more chances there are of success, but also by proportion, the more knockbacks you are likely to get as well. So how resilient are you? How badly do you want it?

Do you flounce, shout or say you will never bother entering again? Not if you want to end up a winner. It was not yours this time around, but the way you handle this perceived failure will determine your future success (although we don't believe it is a failure, as there is always learning in a loss).

So, what should you do? First off, act with dignity. Congratulate the winner.

Commending your opponent for an award well-won is a classy way to handle defeat, and a good habit to develop for all types of competition including business awards. While you probably have a negative knee-jerk reaction to the loss at first, losing gracefully is a valuable life skill and will gain you more recognition as a commendable business leader. Not only is a congratulations to the winner a dignified response, but it is also a positive step in the mental processing of the loss.

It is OK to recognise your disappointment. If you didn't want to win, you wouldn't have entered. Of course it feels disheartening, but you must identify that the disappointment is not about your failure as a person, or the failure of your business. The award was a single opportunity to gain recognition on just one occasion. While you weren't successful in this attempt, there will be others.

Talking about the loss may also help. Success in award entry is about benefitting from your participation in the process, and your successful recovery will require mental understanding of the situation to deal effectively with the feelings of loss. Acknowledging your feelings after the awards competition will enable you to reinforce your commitment to the entry process and the resulting awards. You may choose to make a list of the things you gained from participating. Did it enable you to develop an updated business plan? Did you reconnect with an associate you can form a partnership with? Has it allowed a focus on a future business area? Award entry is both a mental and physical exercise in perseverance and determination. It will test your coping skills but also deliver valuable social interaction opportunities.

Don't disrespect the judging process. This only ever looks like sour grapes and is not an endearing quality for those around you to behold. You may well have seen errors in a process, but if the rules were defined, they were the rules you adhered to. If there is an exceptional miscarriage of the judging process, you may want to write calmly to the judges in the weeks after the event, but don't send off a drink-fuelled email in the late hours that you will only regret when your judgment returns.

> We have witnessed those who have later regretted their post-award rage, and they have acknowledged that they have ruined any chance of future success.

If you are not the winner this time, you have the chance to be a networking ninja instead. Get up from your table and go and meet other people. If six people were up for your award and only one won, four other people are going to be feeling the same as you, so go and introduce yourself to them. Showing how you react in the face of a loss will exhibit your business character, and many non-winners have gained fruitful business opportunities on the night where the result did not go their way. Having seen those who do this successfully, they are effectively able to change a loss into a win and make contacts and deals while the winner is backstage being filmed. Remember that commercial outcome conversations equals new business.

Was there a programme on the table that lists the finalists? Take that opportunity to connect with them via social media, share photos of the event and strengthen your network. Know that competition drives future success. What you learn from this process will drive you forward in the future, so onwards and upwards.

Many competitions will give you a finalist badge or graphic that can be used for your website and often send through a finalist or shortlisted certificate. These are still excellent promotional tools – being a finalist still marks you out as better than others in your industry and should, therefore, be used as a tool for promotion. It is also important to remember that consumers aren't likely to scrutinise an award on what it means and how far you got – if you have been recognised by a big-name award in some way, shape or form, it is enough to be a finalist.

Don't Be Despondent: Sometimes, no matter how great your entry, or how far you stand out from your competition, you won't win. This doesn't mean that your entry or your achievements weren't big or impressive enough, it means that the awards were given in favour of the award sponsors and the industry bodies and media houses that promoted the event.

This section could have gone into the very first chapter about how to find awards or what awards to avoid. However, the truth is, it can be very difficult to know which ones will be biased in favour of their sponsors until you attend the award ceremony itself or find out who won. The problem in distinguishing the good from the bad lies in the fact that almost every award you enter will be sponsored by someone – it is, after all, how those who run the awards make their money, aside from people paying to attend the awards ceremony.

It must also be stated that there are awards where the sponsors are not allowed to enter, or certainly not to be considered in a category that they could influence.

It can be worth researching other people's experience of a particular award as you may find there have been issues before – if this is the case, then avoid entering and look for other awards to enter. However, the majority of the time, it is something you have to accept as part of the award process – as wrong as it may be. We have had experiences where we have attended an award ceremony and the award sponsor won over five categories.

It can be annoying to have paid to attend the ceremony and spent so much time writing the entry, for it all to be seemingly wasted. However, it is vital that this doesn't put you off entering future awards – the majority of awards are not like that, and, even if you do not win but are shortlisted, you will still have a finalist or shortlisted status and badge to use and promote across social media, publications and your website.

Learn From Your Experience: It is important to learn from your experience if you are shortlisted or don't get selected at all. Use your knowledge of entering the awards, as well as the feedback provided after the results were revealed, to make your submission next year even better. Enter again next year but look to improve the evidence you provide against the award criteria and *don't give up*! Winning awards is a numbers game – you have to be in it, to win it and you should enter lots of awards to maximise your chances.

Asking the organisers to give you some feedback is always a good place to start – if an award has had a lot of entries it may not be possible for them to give you feedback, but it is worth asking.

Providing you are writing your awards well, if you enter the same award and award category the following year, the outcome can provide a benchmark for assessing your business's performance.

This will help you to improve faster than your competitors and increase your chances of winning in the future, as you can be actively making changes in your business and award entry process that will help you to stand out and win. Throughout the year, keep a note of everything that happens in your business that is noteworthy or demonstrates your success – it is surprising how many little things you will forget have happened that might be key to catching the judge's eye the next time around.

Be Critical Of Your Submission: It might be the last thing you want to do if you lose, but taking a critical look at your entry will help you to see what went wrong and how you can improve. It can be worth asking the award organisers or judges for their comments, but remember that not every award will be able to do so depending on how many people entered. Looking over your submission, and being critical of your work is a good thing to do if you lose (and when you win). Taking a critical look at your work will let you evaluate where you think you went wrong, what you could have improved upon and what you have done well. Write your findings in a Word document or notebook, making a note of the award category, etc, and look back on your notes when you come to enter future awards.

Compare and Contrast: If you have entered a couple of awards and some have done better than others, compare and contrast them against the award criteria and against each other to understand why one has done better than the other.

Some elements to examine could be:

- Did you include enough solid evidence?

- Did you use too many clichéd phrases, avoid providing solid facts or fail to get to the point?

- Was the entry written well enough? Did you proofread and edit properly?

- Did you follow all of the rules regarding word limits and provide the right supporting material?

- Did you get the right person to write the award? Too much technical language and industry jargon does not go down well with judges.

Even if you don't win, there is always a silver lining – push yourself to make the most of being a finalist. You have got a lot of momentum by being recognised on the shortlist, and when the opportunity is leveraged well, you can make just as much noise as any winner.

Congratulate the other finalists and praise the winner again. Post on social media how thrilled you were to be a finalist, using the event hashtag# and leverage PR opportunities as they present themselves. Try to get a group photo so you can mutually boost each other's business profiles.

Put the finalist logo on your website, email footer and social media as proof of your quality. There is no shame in having a finalist logo on there, and you will find that it won't take long for people to forget that you didn't actually win. Scan your finalist certificate and add to your media file, upload that to your social channels too.

Learn from your experience and ask the judges for their valuable feedback. Use this to understand how you will prepare for the same award next year and have the information ready to improve your submission. Establish your strategy for the next awards – mental preparedness is a crucial component of competing. Implement what you have learned so you can bring your 'A game' to the next entry.

Although uncommon, remember that some 'not-so-ethical' awards are biased toward their sponsors and winners are based upon the advertising spend of nominees. Filter these ones out of your entry calendar and chalk it up to experience. You soon learn which awards to avoid.

Give yourself a consolation prize. Whether or not you win an award, your hard work and participation deserves to be recognised. Maybe a little retail therapy might provide a treat? Acknowledging the journey of the entry process is an excellent way of boosting your mood. Giving yourself credit will not only promote happiness but also give you a stronger sense of control over the situation.

After the dust has settled, you have hopefully taken your time to feel better about the result. Allow yourself the recognition of what you have achieved, then revisit your entry so you can do a critical and non-emotional review of your submission.

It might be that when you read back through your entry, you can immediately see the detail that was lacking, in which case you will not feel so bad about the winner achieving their accolade. It might also be that the businesses in the same category that you entered were very different, and it is therefore difficult to compare. For example, comparing service businesses with manufacturers is always a challenge as a product business has a different ability to scale than a knowledge-based business. There are always going to be different approaches and every business has slightly different challenges to overcome.

What to Do If You Don't Win

After the dust has settled – take your time to feel better about it.

- Be critical of your submission

- What could you have done better?

- What did you do well?

- Did you forget to include something?

- Compare and contrast with the eventual winner to understand what they did well

If you have entered more than one award:

- Have some done better than others?

- Read over them, see what is different

- Write notes on what you can improve for next time

Activity

Review your entry:

- What did I learn?

- What would I do differently next time?

- How can I improve for next time?

Now you are able to look at your entry with greater clarity, look at what you could have done better. Make a list of what you did well and what you would change or add for next time around. Make sure you learn from the knowledge you gained after the submission, as you can constantly evolve your content toward ever more effective entries. Compare and contrast – if you have entered more than one category, have you done better for one classification than you did in the others? Read the submission over again and see what was different and how it matched the judging criteria.

Also, if it is published, read the judges' comments on the winning entries as this will provide valuable insight for next time.

ROAR – What To Do When You Win

The finalist publication has been and gone, you have shared your finalist medal across your social media channels, added it to your website, shared the countdown to the event with the relevant award hashtags and now the day of the awards ceremony is here.

With a fabulous outfit, shining hair and your mobile phone in hand, you attend the gala ceremony. Making your way in the door, you look at the splendour of the room, the lights, the décor, the large stage and the awards laid out, glittering like jewels. Taking your place in front of the sponsors' media wall, you grin for the camera, chat to the other finalists and gaze blankly at the table plan, trying to see your name and where you are sitting. You relax as you see your details against the table number and realise you have a seat and haven't been forgotten.

Arriving at the table, you scan the event programme, again searching for your name, and try to work out when you will know the outcome. Looking longingly at the champagne, you sip carefully and count down the time until your category is announced. The soup arrives and you conduct a masterclass in how not to spill it down your front. You look at the stage hoping you will be doing the walk of fame soon, but also worry about tripping on stage if you actually win.

The awards get underway, maybe with a few words from the sponsors, a video or an activity. But, your concentration is not great – your focus is on the golden envelope and the name contained therein. Rapturous applause greets all the named winners announced thus far, and they look at the audience with delight, collect their prize, pose for photos and utter a few words of gratitude and disbelief before being whisked away to conduct their winner interview.

Then it gets to your section, and the title of the award you entered is announced. The pulse in your neck is now thumping wildly and the other attendees on your table are all holding their breath.

The compere starts to read out the attributes of the winning company. Your heart is thumping harder, it could be you they are talking about. A few words are uttered in your comprehension fog before you realise *yes, it's you* and your name is called out.

You might shriek with delight, hug your partner sitting next to you, or even sit stunned for a while letting the moment sink in. *You are the winner*. It is your time, and the applause is now for you. As you get to your feet, you take the walk of fame, planning your route through the sea of chairs to get to the stage. You thank the sponsor, see your name on the largest screen imaginable and feel the thrill of collecting your trophy and certificate, and maybe you are also presented with a bottle of bubbly. Following your photo call, posing with your prize, you carefully watch your feet to make sure you don't stumble and are escorted onto the stage to the sound of the crowd's cheers. Composing your thoughts quickly, you deliver a wonderful monologue on what the win means to you and your team and how thrilled you are to receive it.

This feeling is unmistakable and quite addictive. Once you have won, you want to win more.

So, how do you make the most of this magnificent occasion? What do you actually do when you have won? Well, you *roar* and you *roar loudly*! You need to shout about the win, what it means to you and how grateful you are. You went through a lot of effort to get this result, so when you have won you need to make some noise.

Write a press release, get the awards' winner logo on to the awards section of your website, put it on your email footer, put it across your social media, create yourself a graphic with a photo of you holding the trophy. There are many things you can do to make that noise. What have past winners done for these awards? What do people usually do in your sector? Do that and then do something different as well. We cover this in detail next.

One of the biggest mistakes award-winners can make is to go to the ceremony, pick up the award, go home and hang it on your wall or in the reception of your business, but do nothing else. There are so many ways you can leverage a win to increase your public profile, improve your sales and grow your business.

Write a press release

A press release can be one of the best ways to get leverage from an award. Depending on the size of the award you have won, your story may be run in national newspapers. However, while this is a possibility, make sure you focus on local publications or publications relevant to your industry as these will be likely to print your news. If you are working with a PR agency, they will likely be able to assist you with writing and distributing a press release, but it is equally possible to create and distribute your own.

Writing a press release is not as difficult as you might think – a press release is designed to give the publication all of the facts and information they could possibly need to create a story. You do not need to be an expert writer or journalist as you are not writing the news story yourself. Think of a press release as a statement rather than a story as it helps to answer the 5 Ws:

- Who – who are the key players? Your company and the award organisation? Who does your news affect? Who does it benefit?

- What – what is new? What has happened?

- Where – where is this happening? Is there a geographical angle? Is the location relevant?

- When – what is the timing of this? Does the timing add significance?

- Why – why is this news important? What does it provide that is different? Why is it worth it for the publication to pick up your story?

Also remember the How! How did this news come about? Did your business do something special to win the award? Have you been implementing new products, services or innovation that have made you newsworthy or contributed to your award win?

These questions are not just useful for a press release after winning an award. Any future press releases for your potential news stories should answer these questions.

While you should not be rigid in the production of your press releases, a simple structure for any press release in five paragraphs as follows:

1. Sums up the entire story in one or two sentences.

2. Puts the story into context. Why is it important?

3. Presents details. Who is involved, and how did the story come about?

4.   Includes a relevant quote to add information, credibility and opinions.

5.   Shows where people can find more details, buy products and get involved.

Once you have written your press release, not only can you send it off to publications, but you can also use the comprehensive, edited content on your website, blog, social media channels and in emails.

It is also important that, once a publication has picked up your story, you don't stop trying to leverage the news. You can link people to the news article on your social media sites or, if it has been printed in a physical publication, take a photo of the article and again, post it to your social media sites. Don't forget to tag the publication as this will give your post an even wider reach.

Don't only put a press release out to the media, put the release on your own website and share that as well. It will depend on who you work with as to whether the media will feature it for a number of factors, but ultimately the easier you make it for the media, the more likely it is to get published. Write a compelling, catchy title for your release and include photos where possible. Create this as an article on your LinkedIn Profile and make sure you add it to your company page as well.

Add it to your website

While your website may not necessarily be your main source of leads, it is absolutely vital that you add the winner or finalist graphic. In a digital world, your website is one of the first places a prospective buyer will go to look for proof of what you do, your quality and your credibility as a company. It is best to create an awards page on your website where you list the awards you have won. You can also have the award on your homepage, as the idea is to make it visible. A potential consumer is unlikely to go out of their way to look for whether you have won an award, but if it is unmissable on your site, it has the potential to make a significant impact on their opinion of your company.

Add your win to your blog or latest updates page on your website – you could use your press release as the basis for this or create something new. Those who are reading your blog are likely to already be interested in your business, so talking about your award win here will reinforce the credibility of your business and could drive a potential customer to make a purchase.

Share across social media channels including both the winner's graphic and photos of the event

Use your own social channels to optimal effect and share the coverage from the award event. Share photos of the ceremony and send congratulatory messages to the other winners and finalists as well. Seek them out and connect with them, build relationships.

On the night you receive your award, it is important to post a photo or update about the event, ensuring that you tag and hashtag relevant terms. However, your social media activity should not stop at the end of the night. Creating another post that thanks the award organisers or a post that shares your press release are further ways to leverage the coverage of the awards in your favour.

Once you have won, or if you were a finalist, you will be sent graphics, or badges that state your placing in the award alongside the name and logo of the award itself. This is something else that you can use in a social media post as well as using the actual images taken on the night.

When you attend the award ceremony, while you probably don't know yet whether you are going to win, it is a good idea to make use of the event itself to increase your visibility online. Try live-tweeting the event, posting updates, congratulating the other winners, posting photos, utilising all the relevant hashtags and engaging with others online while at the event. It is likely that both the award organisers and other guests like yourself will be utilising social media during and after the event. It is important to engage with them as this not only makes you visible to other event attendees, but also to their social media contacts.

Add the award logo/badge to your branding

A major award win is a huge triumph. Put the winner award badge on your branding. You might have opportunities on promotional banners, infographics, or your email footer. Put it on your product packaging if that is relevant as well. An independent award win is a great addition to your advertising material, especially if it is associated with your industry.

What would you choose – a chocolate in a luxury wrapper, or a chocolate that has won a 'Taste' award and has the winner status clearly identified? A winner badge always creates much more impact, makes a visual leap from the shelves and cuts through advertising noise. Think of how a gold medal on a wine bottle might encourage you to select it. If your business has products and it is in keeping with your packaging to do so, put the winner medal out there. Particularly if you have products in shops other than your own, such as in supermarkets, etc, an award logo may be the difference between a customer choosing your brand or going for your competitors.

As well as product packaging, put the badge on your email correspondence, leaflets, price lists and other marketing and advertising material. When someone reads your email or sees your brand on a postcard in their letterbox, your business will be viewed as far more credible and trustworthy because your company has independent validation of its excellence. Customers and potential customers don't have to take your word for it that you are the best.

Including the logos on your branding helps to leverage the win as much as possible, making your hard work pay for itself in the long term.

Send emails to your existing contacts list

You might want to send an email to your database to share your exciting news. If you have a data set that is opted in and GDPR compliant, many of your connections will want to hear about your success, especially if they have helped you to get there. The email update provides a great platform to thank your clients for their support (and is often a great prompt for them to order from you again).

You need to be careful with email data compliance, as most people tend not to like businesses clogging up their email inboxes with news about their business. Unless there is something in it for the recipient, sending an email could potentially have the opposite effect to the positive result you desire. Don't annoy your email contacts list – involve them with the win. Try pairing the news of your win with a discount to celebrate it: "Celebrate with us, enjoy 15% off your next purchase." This is more compelling than: "We've won an award" and it still makes customers and potential clients aware of what you offer.

By matching your win update with a discount code or another deal, you engage people with your news and showcase your award-winning business in a way that will make people notice without annoying them or causing them to want to unsubscribe from your emails. Together, a confirmation of your excellence and a discount have the potential to leverage increased sales or goodwill from your recipients.

While you must take steps to ensure you are not spamming your contacts list with meaningless emails, it can be important to send a communication out about a big award win, as it is unlikely that everyone in your email list will have seen your social media or website posts. Using a press release as a starting point, write a short announcement to your recipients and be sure to include images from the night, the award logo or winner badge and calls to action – to visit your website and to claim a specific discount or promotional offer. It can also be a good idea to include links to your social media accounts within the email, encouraging your clients to see more photos online. This will help the recipients to engage with other channels of communication that you use in your business.

Celebrate with your team

It is very important to celebrate your win with your team. Winning an award is not only an opportunity to build authority with the public and other businesses, it is also a time to foster a sense of achievement among your employees. No person is an island, and it is likely that you haven't achieved a win by your efforts alone, so give a shout out to your team, as they deserve the recognition too. Celebrating an award win with your colleagues will help make them feel part of the bigger picture and show them their skills and expertise are valued. The feeling of inclusiveness will contribute to motivating your team, so they carry on working hard and helping your business on the path to continued success.

Also recognise your wider team – support from a family member, a mentor, your accountant or key suppliers. Your win is their win too, so let them enjoy it as well.

What to Do When You Win

SHOUT about it!

- Write a press release

- Add the logo to an awards section of your website

- Add the logo to your email footer

- Post your press release on your website's blog/latest news page

- Share across your social media channels include the winner awards graphic and photos from the award ceremony

- Send congratulatory messages to the other winners

Take a moment to pause and absorb the achievement. As businesses, we are quick to move on to the next project, and we often don't take the time to commemorate the good stuff. We know that bad things always seem to play on our minds a lot longer, so celebrate the winning moment. Make sure you stop and celebrate with your team, family or your business networking chums, whomever is part of your tribe – let them know they are a valued part of your team.

We asked our winners: What is the most memorable award you have won and why?

Abi Purser:

> I'm proud to say we have won multiple awards – proof that our ethos resonates with so many people. A real standout moment was winning the Guardian's most Innovative Home Business Award in their Business Showcase Awards. The heavyweight judging team, including James Caan from *Dragon's Den*, was impressed by our rapid growth and consistent approach across all our locations. The judges also reflected on how we met the needs and demands of owners for a higher standard of animal welfare and service.

Adeem Younis:

> Perhaps the most memorable recognition is the Prime Minister's Points of Light Award I received at 10 Downing Street. Having the highest office in the country applaud our transforming work was an incredible surprise and honour.

Angela Hughes:

> The most memorable award was the Air Ambulance Lifetime Achievement Award as it meant that my peers recognised my efforts, and working in the same industry, that meant the world to me.

Anna Rabin:

> The Best Business Women Award for Legal Services. Why? Because it is an award judged by a reputable panel of judges who have spent a lot of time and effort going through individual applications in order to sift through and sort out the best.

Catherine Gladwyn:

It has to be the award for best VA book, voted for by VAs.

Darren Clark:

Entrepreneur of the Year, mainly because it was the culmination of all my efforts past and present and yet to come, and I think it's important that we take into account everyone's accomplishments despite background.

James Eades:

We've twice won Apprenticeship Employer of the Year. We're hugely proud of our apprenticeship programme, which we've run now for over 10 years. It has enabled us to develop some real superstars for our team. Winning the first time was amazing, but to win again two years later was recognition of our ongoing commitment.

Jo Macfarlane:

I have been awarded Plastic Free Champion in my town from Surfers Against Sewage. It means so much to be able to raise awareness of issues facing the current climate.

Julie Grimes:

I was finalist in the Best Business Women Awards in three categories: Recruitment Services, Customer Service and Most Inspiring Business Woman. I won Recruitment Services which is my most memorable award (and the one I was really wanting to achieve), due to the competition being larger recruitment agencies and some trading longer, which makes you feel it couldn't be you.

Laura Birrell:

The Great British Entrepreneur Award – Entrepreneur of the Year for Scotland and Northern Ireland. This was the first award that I won so that feeling of winning was amazing. I didn't see how I could possibly win an award. The feeling I had, to have achieved such a significant award as my first, will always stay with me.

Lynn Stanier:

Being nominated for, and receiving an MBE for Community Services to Sri Lanka from Her Majesty the Queen at Windsor Castle will be the most memorable and biggest honour of my life.

Natasha Penny:

The Small Business of the Year Award. The event was arranged by the Small Biz 100 and the Small Business Saturday team, and sponsored by Facebook. I was awarded not only the At Your Service Award, but also the overall Small Business of the Year! I still to this day cannot believe my little business, based in rural Wiltshire, received this outstanding award.

Rachel Spratling:

Best Client Results for the South West. It was fantastic to celebrate a client who had experienced a 300% increase in turnover, and a 400% increase in profit as a result of the work we had done together.

Ray Dawson:

Charity of the Year. It was a personal ambition fulfilled after three years of building credibility and it means the world to me and to our charity.

Sam Bramley:

South West Female Entrepreneur of the Year. To be recognised in that category with so many other women I respect was huge.

Sam Gooding:

Winning Wiltshire Community Business of the Year on the 25th Anniversary Awards was a huge achievement and a big reward for every member of our team.

Simon Crowther:

Being included on the Forbes 30 Under 30 Industry list. The list is designed to identify leaders of the Next Generation. I was on the line-up alongside truly amazing individuals. The Forbes List was a distinct turning point where I was taken more seriously, and my company became one of the most highly respected flood defence companies both in the UK and overseas. I was even invited to open the London Stock Exchange with Forbes.

Simon Buck:

Best Client Feedback three years on the trot. Awards that are totally independent and based only on NPS scores (net promotor scores) mean the world to me.

Tracey Smolinski:

Being Sales Rep of the Year – a very proud moment.

The PR Benefits of Entering an Award
by Fiona Scott

Fiona has been a journalist for more than 30 years working in print, radio and television. She is still a working journalist and has her own media consultancy that supports businesses, individuals, charities and organisations to become more visible through the media, and social media.

As a storyteller, she helps others tell their own business stories, so we asked her to explain how to leverage the public relations benefits from award winning and what a journalist will *actually* want to know about you and your business. Over to Fiona to explain what the media requires.

If you are truly embracing public relations in your business or organisation, sooner or later you will be discussing entering an award initiative of some kind. It could be local, regional, national and it might be centred around a particular community or business sector.

Why will this subject come up? Public relations involves storytelling in multiple different ways and that means you have to do stuff to write stories about. It sounds simple, however, public relations is all about marketing and it's something you must keep doing. These days where we can receive information from all angles all day and night, one story isn't going to cut it. You should have a story plan – and in your plan can be the relevant awards opportunities available during any given year.

Awards can be very effective because their legacy can go far beyond the actual shortlisting or winning of a particular title or accolade. Awards enhance your credibility, they can be the key which gets you before that potential client, or journalist who has 10 potential contributors and makes you stand out. Often an award gives people confidence in you, your service or your product.

If you are going to enter an award, you have to consider it as a PR project. Entering is not enough. You have to be ready to act and be truly engaged in the process.

You have to consider multiple things:

- Are you entering and answering the required questions properly and in enough depth?

- Do you have to pay to enter?

- Is it an awards event where I'll have to buy a ticket?

- What should I wear?

- Should I take my team?

- How should they behave at the event?

- How do I use this as a PR hook?

The PR hooks are the subject of focus here. First of all, you entering awards is *not* a story. It becomes a story when you are shortlisted as a finalist. At that point a story in your community, and perhaps in the trade press (if it's a sector or specialist awards event), is relevant.

Send out your story to local and trade journalists *with a good colour image* of your team – never black and white, and never less than 1MB in resolution. Be clear what the awards are, the category you have been shortlisted in and the project if that is relevant. Remember this is a press release so there is no guarantee your story will be used. If you want a guarantee you need to buy advertorial space. However, it is likely a media outlet of some kind in your area will run the story, especially if you have included a good picture.

Sometimes judges will hold an event to question the finalists or may even visit you and your premises. Ask for permission to evidence their visit on social media – once again this shows you are engaged in the process. Share the pictures once permission is granted. This activity can be done on a phone or tablet, tag the name of the business the judge works for, and build them into your story.

Prior to the awards night, think about how to maximise the PR – is there a hashtag for the event? If so, start communicating on social media using that hashtag, also tag the name of the sponsors. This shows before you have even arrived, that you are part of that conversation, that tribe, that group of people. Connect with and follow anyone also using that hashtag positively. That way you will know people before you have even stepped into the room. Evidence your attendance on the night via social media and also share the posts of others in the room if they are positive. Avoid negative chatter, it's not good for you or your brand.

Consider photographs for the night – is there a professional photographer? If so, can you get an image featuring you? How quickly can you get it? Do you have to pay for it or is it gifted to you? Be sure of the parameters and be ready to act on them if you win. You need to be very clear you want to use any images for your own marketing purposes including sending out a press release.

If this is not allowed, consider hiring a professional photographer to bring with you – or have one on standby. While it can be rare to do this, you could hire one the day after and get brighter daylight images when low light at a night time venue was an issue. If you do not like the official image, you could get one taken yourself with your trophy. Whatever photography you use, do it quickly – certainly within the week before the story becomes old.

Be aware, award ceremonies in the evening are generally held in low light venues and the images can appear very blue or purple. It is often the case that those taken on a phone or a tablet are simply not good enough for use by the media. Selfies are definitely not suitable. So if there is an official photographer, make sure you get featured in the shot and get their contact details, so you have a means to follow up with them.

A second story is relevant if you win. At the point of winning do any media interviews available on the night and make that a priority over celebrating with your team. A journalist or press photographer may have several jobs to do that evening and they won't want to be hanging about. Consider what you want to say beforehand. Have this in your mind prior to any win and remember a journalist can take notes on what you say on the rostrum so think about your tone and language. Think also about the behaviour of your team. You are there to showcase and celebrate your team and brand, so prior to the event set some boundaries around acceptable behaviour.

A team which has clearly had a lot of alcohol and is messing about or swearing and making any kind of scene can damage your reputation and that of your business. People will be polite on the night, however, they may think twice about working with you. If that's a risk, go to the awards by yourself or with a very small group. Journalists who are allowed to attend the event are also free to report on anything which happens at that event, good or bad, so be mindful of that and keep an eye on your behaviour and that of your team.

A journalist may come from a local paper or niche press and take their own image. Note 'their own image' – that doesn't mean you don't send out your own press release. Most areas have more than one media organisation, on or offline, so simply send out your story anyway. However, don't send it to the journalist who did turn up. Forget them, they've already got it covered.

If no media is present, and that is often the case, be your own journalist. Write a simple story about your win, include the picture you have and be clear you have permission to use it. Send that in to your local paper or trade press. Take the winning logo, which should be sent to you, and add that to your email and any printed literature around your business. Put details in your next newsletter and celebrate the win with your social media audience. The tone should be 'humble and grateful' never 'we deserve this because we are wonderful'.

Sometimes awards events are actually run by a local media outlet such as a local paper. With that will come other things: lots of extra coverage and usually a much-reduced advertising package. This is worth taking up to show you are committing to this and really going for it, and you'll sit alongside others with similar ambitions that they are willing to invest in. Do not do this half-heartedly. Think of it as an all or nothing situation.

If, during this process, a journalist gets something wrong – describes your business incorrectly or spells your name wrong – that's not defamation so don't get on your high horse about it. A mistake is simply that, a mistake. Defamation is something else entirely and involves substantial risk to you as a person. Mistakes do happen. If it happens to you, call them up with a positive tone and explain that there's been an error and ask what can be done to put it right. Put the ball in their court.

Often it means you'll get more coverage given freely because you've approached the issue with a positive mindset.

Do remember that it is unusual to win first time around – so don't be disheartened. Being shortlisted is both a story and a win in itself. If you do win, the next time around you will often not be eligible to enter again. Don't be discouraged. Look for other award opportunities and perhaps offer to be a judge or a sponsor next time. That way you become part of the conversation anyway, and you also get visibility around that role. Just be very clear from the outset what the time commitment will be.

After that high has dissipated don't forget, when engaging with the media, to always include a sentence that mentions your win. This will stay current for about two years. Such a win will give confidence to journalists that you are credible, as they will know you won as a result of the judgment of a panel or through a voting process. It may be the one thing that sets you apart. It can also lead to speaking opportunities if that's of interest to you. We see it all the time. It becomes a reason to talk to you, it builds on your reputation and you find that people take you more seriously in your sector and in your community.

In terms of the media, it gives a journalist confidence that they can come to you to comment on particular matters or issues that can come up again and again – this could be related to a business issue or an issue that affects your sector. Examples of this might be: "Can you comment on what the Budget means for small businesses?" or "Can you comment on the new government legislation and the effect on your sector?" Once journalists know that you are media-friendly, they will seek you out for comment. An award can, over time, bring the media to you and this can be true of national media too.

One final thought on this – if you work the opportunity, it can also generate a strong feelgood factor within your team. This is often widely overlooked and underestimated. However, a team likes to be valued and rewarded. They like to know that their hard work is recognised and doing this outside the work environment can be very productive.

My advice would be to engage staff in the process too – ask them to keep an eye out for other awards initiatives which may be of interest or relevance to the business. Do a debrief with them of what worked and what wasn't so good, so you are better prepared for the next time. Getting 'buy in' from the team is hugely powerful and means you can even set targets for each person on the night, for example, ensure you talk to everyone on table 1, you talk to everyone on table 2 and get their cards, etc. Ensure your team follow up on those connections within the week, while the feeling is still fresh.

To recap – awards are good for PR because:

- It's a story if you are shortlisted

- It's a story if you win

- It adds to your credibility in the community or sector

- It can bring the media to you for comment on matters affecting your community or sector

- It can allow you to network with businesses or organisations you might not otherwise meet

- It can become a point in the year to start a gentle sales process with the other attendees – guests, finalists, sponsors and judges

- It provides social proof of your competence

- It can be the hook that gets you speaking opportunities for increased visibility

- It increases brand awareness

Thank you to Fiona for that valuable insight as a journalist. It always makes sense to give the media what they want in a format that they can easily use. Being the go-to person will build your media credibility and increase future opportunities.

A Final Word – Is It Worth It?

If you have made it this far, I am sure we have had a chance to convince you of the benefits of entering and winning awards for your business, but in case we haven't, many past winners have described the benefits they have personally experienced in winning awards for their businesses.

Caroline:

Gaining credibility has been the main thing. We have all our certificates displayed on our own wall of fame, so when potential licensees come to visit it gives them reassurance. Once you win you can use the logo on your website – a great reason for award winning.

Roni:

It's had an impact on me and ultimately on the profile of my business. It's a confidence booster, which ultimately also builds your credibility.

We also asked our winners if they had had unexpected outcomes from winning awards, for example, TV appearances.

Roni:

It's all a bit of a whirlwind. I have had lots of TV and newspaper opportunities from winning various awards because of their PR companies who also have connections to various media parties – it's been great.

Caroline:

As a winner, we have had the chance to have our photo taken with celebrities!

So ultimately, would they recommend awards entry to other businesses?

Roni:

Absolutely, absolutely. Yes, definitely 100%, 110% even. It's great, it's an opportunity to raise your profile and that of your business while also inspiring others. I am mentoring a number of young females – they know that I've won these awards and they say it's something that they can look up to also. It's just fantastic, it really is.

Caroline:

I would definitely recommend it, I think it's something that people can find a little scary, but actually when you look at doing your first entry for an award, you have to really think about it… and it does get slightly easier the more you do. The applications often ask very similar questions.

It can be time-consuming, which is why you need to choose which ones you enter, but I would definitely recommend it – for us it has resulted in attracting customers and licensees. For other companies, it might be that they are looking at an exit strategy, or investment, then the profile created could really help. On a day-to-day basis, it can help with getting customers through the door. It's really good for staff morale when you win awards, because it celebrates everyone's input.

There are also some unusual awards, where there can be prizes other than the certificate and the trophy. We won a trade mission to China that was a result of the HP Export awards. Sometimes it's just the credibility and a trophy you win but sometimes you can win support for your business, whether that's financial support or mentoring support or trade missions. It is worth looking, depending on your industry, at sector specific awards that might offer you an opportunity to build your credibility among your peers.

Julianne Ponan, owner and CEO of Creative Nature, knows what it takes to build and run a successful business. Among her awards are Forbes 30 Under 30, Guardian Leader of the Year and being the youngest winner of the National NatWest Everywoman Artemis Award for Women Entrepreneurs.

Julianne:

One of the greatest aspects of award entry is the chance to inspire others. I enjoy sharing both the trials and triumphs of business and, as an entrepreneur, it is important to share on the entry form what you have learned and how you have recovered, as well as what has gone well within the business.

Awards have also given us the platform to raise awareness about food allergies, so we can contribute to discussions across our broader society of the issues we are passionate about. Winning awards gives you a voice in the media and can be a great way to raise your personal profile for speaking engagements and even appearing on TV. Being recognised enables you to gain more credibility in your industry, which is why entering your business is so important to give you future opportunities. After winning the FSB Small Business of the Year 2018, my business Creative Nature was then invited to open the London Stock Exchange. This was an incredible boost to the team.

Wilfred Emmanuel-Jones, founder of The Black Farmer, provides the following insight:

> There are tonnes of awards out there. When I first started my business, The Black Farmer, the key thing was getting credibility among the retailers, and a way to do this was winning awards.
>
> Until you are endorsed by others, it is a bit of a struggle. What we did was enter everything – you have to be confident; you have to have a product that can win and you have to know your competition.
>
> Even 15 years later, we still enter competitions. It is still seen as something that endorses what you do. I think people should see entering awards as part of their marketing budget. When you are talking to buyers, you will have a lot more credibility because it is more than what your feelings are – it is based on independent views and a testament that is approved by an independent body of people.
>
> We have won many awards, but it is still a good way for our hard work to be endorsed. It justifies the effort. Each one is unique; they are important as you are being awarded for achievement – it is a vital independent endorsement.

We asked our winners, what their top tips are for other award entrants.

Abi Purser:

> Back everything up with a successful and coherent business case. Judges want to hear what your USP is and how that came about. They can see how my love of animals and desire

to be the best of the best has translated into the business they see before them. Judges want your story – show them why you are relevant in today's economy.

Adeem Younis:

Don't be shy. Awards inspire your staff and raise the standard of your industry. Buck the trend, try something different and stand out from the crowd.

Angela Hughes:

This is your time to blow your own trumpet – don't be modest.

Angela Hicks:

Read the criteria and answer the questions properly.

Anna Rabin:

If at first you don't succeed, don't be beaten and keep trying. Not winning does not mean you aren't a winner, and it will happen at the right time.

Catherine Gladwyn:

Other business owners are unbelievably supportive, so don't think twice about asking for votes – people really do love to help.

Darren Clark:

Don't be afraid to show yourself for who you are. Show your accomplishments in their fullest, but also what you are still working hard to achieve. No one is the finished perfect article.

James Eades:

> Award entries are no place to be humble or modest – it's important to stand out, be punchy and succinct and make sure your winning qualities are obvious.

Jo Macfarlane:

> Sometimes you are so close to the business it takes fresh eyes to really see your accomplishments. Don't be afraid to hire some qualified help to apply for you.

Julie Grimes:

> Leave enough time to read the questions properly and answer them within the guidelines. I would say at least four weeks. Stick to the word count and gather evidence. Enter with 100% commitment.

Laura Birrell:

> Don't be shy about mentioning all your achievements, including personal impact, to get you to where you are. Winning an award is showing how you have gone further than others to stand out from the crowd

Lynn Stanier:

> Go for it! Although it is advisable to plan your entry well in advance.

Natasha Penny:

> Believe in yourself, be honest, and share the things you are doing regardless of how small, as they all make the world and business a better place.

Rachel Spratling:

You've got to be in it, to win it!

Ray Dawson:

Be proud and tell your story – make it like a picture painted in words. The beautiful picture describes you, your dream, your business or your charity.

Sam Bramley:

Be engaging in your answers. Use language to keep the reader interested.

Sam Gooding:

Make sure you take time and effort to catch the judge's eye. Shine, always be yourself and proud of what you have achieved – don't ever let anyone put you off or drag you down.

Simon Crowther:

Enter any competition you can – even just filling in an entry form is a great opportunity to see how far you've come. Make sure your passion comes across. People now see being an entrepreneur as a fashionable thing, but you need to have the passion of why you actually started your business. What is your business's story? What financial information is there to back it up? Find out who the judges are and connect with them on LinkedIn, keep posting regularly and they will subconsciously be aware of who you are and what you do.

Simon Buck:

My biggest tip would be to enter. Too many people wait for perfect, forgetting just how much they have achieved. Entering will force you to reflect and realise the achievements.

Tony Robinson:

> Enter awards programmes where you respect, trust and are, frankly, impressed by the calibre of the judges. It is really the calibre of the judges that influences how others perceive your award and recognise the major achievement. It is one of the reasons why the GB Entrepreneurs Awards are so successful. We're a proud community of judges, all entrepreneurs, and the very best entrepreneurs in the UK will enter the awards because they trust in us to judge well.

> Do not to try to bluff or fib your way to success – judging criteria is well-honed, and facts rather than fantasy win every time.

> Look carefully at the awards lunch or evening event. Is it the kind of event that the busiest and most successful people in your sector or profession are likely to attend? Unusual venues attract the big names.

Tracey Smolinski:

> Standout, be different, be bold, believe in yourself, make an impact and difference to other people's lives and have a strong purpose.

Thank you to all our wonderful winners, judges and award ceremony organisers for sharing their knowledge.

> Of course, alongside our winners, I also believe in the benefits of winning awards, otherwise I would not have written a book to help you succeed as well. Many of my clients have recognised our award wins as a key selection criteria, and apart from the ongoing jokes about having to get a larger awards cabinet (yes, we can do that), they have been very supportive and congratulatory.

At a networking event recently, a connection said: "I have not seen any award photos from you for a few weeks – have you been on holiday?!" It is all good-natured and shows how much 'cut through' from general social media noise winning an award can present.

We are delighted that you have taken the opportunity to win for your business so seriously. Please keep in touch and email denise@purpolmarketing.co.uk with your winning images and stories.

Tales From the Ceremony

Falling on the stage, mismatched shoes, tripping on your dress and spilling soup down your front – award ceremonies can provide a host of challenges as well as delights. Here is a selection of our favourite moments, as well as a few we can gladly say did not happen to us.

Before I allow you to enjoy a few magical memories from fellow award winners, I would love to share a couple of my own moments.

So what was the story that I mentioned earlier about being serenaded by Mr 'GoCompare' Wynne Evans?

I was at the Great British Entrepreneur Awards and the category that I had entered and was a finalist for was the Go-Do Entrepreneur of the Year. I looked in the programme, and this was the first category featured so would be the first award to be announced.

I was sitting at the table with Oli Barratt, influential entrepreneur and start-up mentor, excitedly anticipating the results. All heads turned to the stage as the ceremony started and the finalists' names were called. Everyone cheered all of the finalists as they were announced, and then the winners name was read out – and it was me!

I hugged and kissed my husband, wobbled to my feet and made my way to the stage, being sure not to trip up in my heels in a full-length purple gown.

I was given the fabulous trophy and had a stage selfie, and after the applause, I left the stage in a daze… only to be called back to much laughter as I did not realise that I was also due my certificate and champagne. On my walk back on to the stage for a second time with everyone shouting 'come back, Denise!' Wynne serenaded me with *'This is your moment; This is your time'* in his finest operatic voice. That moment will be engraved on my memory for ever (and all the other winners were probably glad that I had gone first, because then they knew the drill!).

At the Best Business Women Awards, I had another 'moment' though thankfully the audience was limited. It had been raining and I exited the ceremony with a magnificent heavy crystal trophy (back in its padded foam-lined box), my framed certificate and the awards goody bag.

Chatting to another awards winner (about shoes), I appeared to forget I had heels on. The first stumble caught my dress lining and with the second step, I had nowhere to go apart from the concrete floor.

My first and only thought was to save the trophy.

As I crashed down on to the concrete floor, I heard something smash. On this occasion I was thankful that it was the picture frame with my certificate in, which was in the goody bag, not the crystal trophy. In a move beloved of many goalkeepers, I had managed to keep the trophy in its box aloft, and instead smashed down on the side of my hand.

Back on my feet and embarrassed, I looked down at my hands – one was bleeding across my palm and the other was already swelling. I spent the rest of the night with both hands in ice buckets (but most importantly the trophy was fine!).

It appears I am not alone in creating memorable award moments – here is motivational speaker and award-winning coach, Taz Thornton, sharing her story: "What They Didn't Know About My Stride Of Pride".

Over to Taz:

People still comment on my bold strides toward that stage, even now. What they saw was a woman stomping, with purpose, to pick up that trophy – stopping along the way to hug one of the other finalists. However, the truth is a little different from the picture I apparently painted that evening.

It was 11 October 2018. It would have been my dad's 86th birthday. When he died, back in 2006, a little of my world died with him. My dad, Eric Walter Thornton, had just come home from hospital. It was October, not long before his birthday. I remember being really happy that he was on the mend.

I was away in York and called home that evening. I expected to end up chatting to my mum, but she was out consoling my aunt who'd recently lost her husband. And so, the rarity happened: my dad, who usually answered the phone, only to pass the handset to my mother, stayed on the phone and talked. We even exchanged I love you's. For a man who didn't really start to show his emotions until his later years (I remember being really surprised the first time he hugged me without being asked, or it being the obligatory farewell embrace before I left after a visit), hearing those three tiny-huge words, unprompted, was a real gift. He told me he was proud of me too. It was a beautiful, treasured communication.

The following morning, the call came to tell me he'd left this world. He'd been poorly overnight, and he was dead by the time the ambulance arrived. I remember my wife driving us back to the hotel and packing our things in a daze. I remember calling work and robotically telling them that my father had passed away and I'd need to take time off. I remember nothing being quite the same after that.

The death of my dear old dad was one of those pivotal moments. It led in to the series of catastrophic life lessons that would take me into a breakdown and, ultimately, transform into the breakthrough that resulted in completely reinventing my life. Without that exact set of circumstances, I might never have shed those corporate handcuffs and set off into the brave, new world of self-employment. I might never have spent a decade or so learning from shamans and medicine people, trained in NLP, fire walking, mentoring, or gathered all those empowerment teachings. I might never have become a coach, and I most certainly wouldn't have been sitting at the Best Business Women Awards, having been nominated in the category of Best Coach.

And that brings us nicely back to the point of this chapter.

Even getting the invite to that awards night was something of a surprise for me. You see, I hadn't nominated myself. My wife, Asha, had been secretly collaborating with some of my clients and, between them, they'd put together what must have been a cracking entry. Obviously, by the time the awards evening arrived, I knew I'd made it through to the finals but, in all honesty, I didn't believe I'd make it any further.

I was so convinced that I created all sorts of stories to fit my belief. You see, in my old life, at the top of the corporate tree in the publishing world, I was involved in several big, posh awards ceremonies. I'd done everything from the judging to the table planning to the compering on the night, so I thought I knew how these things worked. Or, at least, I was a little flexible with my knowledge to further convince myself I hadn't won.

I was there with my wife and one of our friends, Sally, and when we checked the table plan and saw we were at the back of the room, that was all the proof I needed that I could kick back and relax. "See?" I said to them both, "We're right at the back. We wouldn't be right at the back if we'd won." Secretly, I was so nervous. I just needed a reason to chill out.

As it would have been my dad's birthday, I decided to celebrate and enjoy the night in his honour. That meant doing something that, for me, was quite unusual. I ordered a drink. In day-to-day life, I'm not quite, but almost, teetotal. I'm on the road a lot, plus I do quite a lot of energy work, so alcohol and I aren't the best of friends. This night, though, I was making an exception to toast my dad. I ordered a vodka and cranberry. Double.

I hadn't accounted for 'easy' hotel measures. I'm pretty sure it was a glass full of vodka with a tiny splash of cranberry. I did a bit of mingling, saw another coach I knew who was up for the same award and had a bit of chit-chat. She'd been a finalist the year before and jokingly announced that if I won, she'd kill me. Oh, how we laughed. I reassured her that I hadn't won and that she had it in the bag this time. Seated at my table, someone bought me another 'gigantavodka' and cranberry, and I relaxed into the evening, chatting to the others we were sitting with. It was a lovely, fun, night. A little way in, I felt something untoward happen!

As this was a special occasion, I'd pushed the boat out a bit with my outfit. I hadn't really worn heels since my corporate days, but I'd bought a new pair for the night, as well as splashing out on a designer dress and, of course, the underwear required for such a number. Spanx. The underwear that sucks you in, in all the right places, and takes about a week to get on and even longer to get off. I'd gone for one of those numbers with the press studs in the worst place possible. Like one of those awful body suits that were in during the 80s and 90s and, for some ill-conceived reason, seem to be making a comeback today. There I sat, feeling nicely warm, vodka flowing through my veins, when I felt those press studs come undone.

Pop. Pop. Pop. Then a really awkward sense of freedom in my nether regions! I shuffled around in my seat. The awards were in full swing. Would it be really poor manners to zip off to the ladies and button myself back up? I squirmed for a few more moments, then whispered to my wife: 'It's a while before my award yet, isn't it?' She nodded and shushed me. Bless. I whispered into her ear that I was zipping to the restroom and carefully stood up.

It was at precisely that moment that the compere announced: 'And next we have Best Coach.' I sat back down. I hadn't won. All would be fine. As they started talking about the winner, it gradually dawned on me that they were talking about *me*. Sally still laughs at my sweary table reaction, though, of course, she didn't realise my delicate predicament.

As I stood and began the long walk to the stage, there were only three thoughts going through my mind:

1. Dad, if you had anything to do with this, thank you, but you could have warned me not to down two double gigantavodkas when I'm wearing new heels.

2. I need to check in with my fellow coach so she doesn't actually kill me.

3. Oh. My. God. My Spanx are undone!

It transpires that the determined stride of pride that people comment on was actually just me trying to stay upright and keep it all together, when my Spanx were flapping about between my thighs like a couple of windsocks in a thunder storm. To this day, I cringe when I think back to the only words I said to my fellow coaches as we all gathered for a group picture minutes later. Still in shock, still wondering how on earth I was the one clutching the sparkly trophy, the only words that came were: 'My Spanx just popped!'

If you were there on that evening, and that was your first impression of me, I can only apologise. I'm much less bizarre when I'm not being compressed by Lycra with all the strength of an angry boa constrictor and worrying about all that air circulating in places it really shouldn't be while wearing a short dress!

Humour aside, the impact of being declared Best Coach in 2018 was far-reaching. I already enjoyed a successful practice, but the publicity on the back of that accolade really did create a very definite spike in interest, and my waiting list grew longer as a result.

If you've been thinking about taking part, I'd highly recommend it – it's a brilliant event, beautifully organised, and there's a wonderful networking circuit on the back of it too. I will always look back on my awards night with a smile. My crystal trophy sits on our bookcase in the living room and, every time the sun hits it at just the right angle, I like to think that's my dad, winking at me and, perhaps, raising a ridiculously large vodka in my direction.

Unbeknown to Taz, I had shared this very experience – though thankfully not the malfunctioning undergarments! I won my first national award – the Best Independent Consultant, from the Women in Marketing Awards on the anniversary of my mother-in-law's passing, making an emotional occasion just that bit more so.

There are many tales from award ceremonies that can provide inspiration – let's hear from some winners on what their special moments were.

Abi Purser:

> We won bronze in the Hotel and Leisure category of the National Family Business Awards. It's a national award and was a special moment to reflect on how far we had come. Winning a Family Business Award specifically meant a lot to me as we really pride ourselves on being a family business. It's incredible how our Longcroft family has grown from strength to strength over the past few years, which makes me feel enormously proud. The team believe passionately in treating their feline guests as part of the family, placing the customer and their cats at the heart of every decision and offering them a home-from-home experience.

Angela Hughes:

> I did feel emotional when I was invited to a meeting of the ambulance trust AGM in 2010 and, unbeknown to me, the Chief Executive had organised a special NHS award for me in recognition of my outstanding contribution to pre-hospital care.

Angela Hicks:

> I felt emotional at all the awards where I had been nominated by peers but particularly when I won the Property Personality of The Year Award as it was completely unexpected, and I had been nominated by people in a different industry.

Jo Macfarlane:

> I was able to prove you can be a winner even when you don't take home the trophy. I was able to take the walk of fame to the stage anyway... having won the bingo shout out. It is all about positive attitude!

Julie Grimes:

> When my name was called out as the winner from the shortlist at the Best Business Women Awards, my husband jumped up before me and cheered so loudly everyone thought he had won it! He had tears of pride running down his cheeks.

Lynn Stanier:

> Everyone on my table reached for their lipstick just in case their name was called out in readiness for the winners' photo... I didn't, as I had absolutely no thoughts at all of winning. I regretted it as I walked toward the stage and nervously mumbled an apology for wearing no lipstick as I received my award!

Ray Dawson:

> When I first sent in the entry, I had total belief in the worthiness of Waste Not Want Not to win. Could the little guys come out on top? Those magic words came out: "And the winner is Waste Not Want Not". I wanted to cry, and up we went to receive the award. As we approached the stage, I was overcome with pride that we had done it. On the Monday, we called a meeting and announced to our team of volunteers that we had won! I had the trophy in a bag under my arm. Then in walks a volunteer with a surprise birthday cake, and I clapped without thinking, followed shortly by the sound of breaking glass. So I looked at the thousand pieces

of glass and said: "It's OK guys, nothing a bit of superglue won't fix". The replacement now has pride of place in the showroom.

Simon Crowther:

One of my favourite aspects has been meeting like-minded entrepreneurial individuals. As an entrepreneur, it's easy to feel isolated, and therefore meeting driven individuals who face similar issues has been invaluable. This is one aspect I never appreciated when entering awards. The networking opportunities are fantastic and should not be missed.

Wendy Griffith:

I waddled up to the stage to receive my Best Networker at the Business Women Awards at 39 weeks pregnant, all the time worrying that I may go into labour from the shock of winning it! My labour did start that night!

Summary Of Learning On How To Win Awards

Do you want to be a winner? Here is a quick review of all the main themes in the book:

Why bother?

Key message: there is an award for everyone

- Gain competitive advantage

- Achieve independent validation

- Generate free PR

- Boost team morale

- Secure trust in your business

What award types are on offer?

- International and national

- Regional and local

- By sector, e.g. construction

- By role, e.g. architect

- By demographic, e.g. gender

First steps for entry

- **Choosing which awards to enter**

When choosing, there is lots to consider:

- o Which awards are relevant to your business?

- o Which awards offer the best pay back?

- o What are the costs attached, including time and energy as well as financial?

- o Do you fit the criteria?

- **Choosing a category**

Consider a more obscure category that will have fewer candidates in the running.

- **Practical elements of submission**

Practicalities such as deadlines may affect your decision on which awards to enter.

- **Have you got what it takes?**

Almost certainly yes, provided you choose the right award for your company and dedicate the time to write a compelling entry. There is a myth that only big companies win awards, but this is not true, and you have to be in it to win it.

- **Visualise**

What are you hoping to achieve? Visualising can help make it a reality.

Planning and research

1. Research

   Why is this important? At this stage, knowledge really is power. Look toward trade association sites, industry bodies, chambers of commerce, media houses, newsletters, competitor websites and so on, to do your research.

2. Plan ahead

   Schedule upcoming entries for the next year – which awards do you plan to enter? Prioritise and set aside time.

3. Gather evidence

   Facts, figures, quotes, graphs and photos will all help your entry stand out and evidence why you should win. Don't recycle from other award entries, the criteria is unlikely to be the same.

4. Plan

   Write early, do your homework, plan your headings and subheadings or bullet point your answers first if that helps.

Writing your entry

1. The 5 Ws

   What, who, when, where and what's in it for me?

2. Time management

   Time management is essential – schedule dates for drafting and editing.

3. Writing style

   Short, easy to read paragraphs are best and make use of headings, subheadings, etc, to ensure your entry is as clear as possible.

4. What to include

   Award winning is essentially communication, connection, value and selling at the final stage. Focus on benefits-led messaging.

5. Stand out

   Use headings, subheadings, appropriate colours, photos and graphs to both evidence criteria, but also to stand out. The judges will appreciate an interesting entry that is different from the rest they have to read.

6. Stick to the rules of submission

   Deadlines, word and page counts, font, etc. It helps to pick the right person for the job, and you should always write offline before uploading your entry into the online portal.

7. Understand audience needs

   Proofread more than once, provide facts and figures to help them out, be honest and don't avoid specific areas as they will notice, and explain in simple terms what your business does.

8. Maximising your chances

   Showcase strategic thinking, detail how you have adapted to events, provide financials that evidence core growth, provide examples of innovation and improvements, make the most of word and page count for each question, keep it all relevant, use testimonials and endorsements, and start early as compiling an effective entry takes time.

9. Proofread

Have someone else proofread your work and provide them with the marking scheme and questions.

Your audience

- Who are they?

    o Technical experts, procurement professionals, sponsors and celebrities – consider their expectations.

- Make it simple for them

    o Write a clear, concise response, use headings, present the document as requested, reference all attachments and respond promptly to requests.

- What are they looking for?

    o Judges want to see how your business leads in the industry and the methods you have used to improve. Tell the story of your business: what industry challenges, business obstacles and personal trials have you confronted? How have you overcome these?

- Win themes

    o Tell a story with positive language, take the assessor on a journey.

After submission – if you are unsuccessful

- Congratulate the winner

- Make the most of being a finalist

    o Being a finalist can leverage as much PR and opportunity as a win. Featuring a finalist logo on your website is still proof of quality.

- Learn from the experience

  o Ask for feedback and measure how far you get in the award year on year.

- Make it easier for yourself next time

  o Create a database of information, with evidence and keywords in the format of an award entry that you can refer back to next time.

After submission – if you win

- Press release
- Use the award logo
- Create momentum on social media
- Congratulate other winners
- Celebrate with your team and your customers with a promotion

Where to find awards

- Google
- Industry bodies
- Websites
- Newsletters
- Blogs
- Trade association websites
- Chambers of commerce
- Media houses

Summary of learning

- Build an awards target list

- Build an awards entry content database

- Choose the right awards depending on relevance and credibility

- Keep track of progress and revisit old entries to provide good examples of your best practice

- Get feedback and constantly update your information

Need More Help?

Let us write your entry!
Contact denise@purpolmarketing.co.uk and we can help.

Summary of Learning

Summary of Learning

- Build an award target list

- Choose the right awards / category – what gives greatest credibility?

- Create an awards entry content library

- Get feedback and constantly update your information

Contact Details

Denise O'Leary

Email	Denise@purpolmarketing.co.uk
Telephone	07966 333657
	01249 481411
Role	Managing Director and Founder – Purpol Marketing
LinkedIn	https://www.linkedin.com/in/denise-o-leary-ma-chartered-marketer-85610389/
Facebook	/PurpolMarketing
Twitter	@PurpolMarketing

About The Author

Denise O'Leary was born in Trowbridge, Wiltshire, and retained her love of the countryside, now living in Chippenham with her husband, Malc, and a large selection of wildlife including their beloved hedgehogs.

Denise launched Purpol Marketing in 2014, as a home-based business offering brand, marketing and bid strategy consultancy specialising in the manufacturing and construction industries. From railway brake engineering via plastic drainage to construction, Denise saw the marketing 'fluff' delivered by some agencies and wanted to offer credible, hard-headed and logical suggestions to clients that actually work. Denise spotted a gap in the market for a tailored service for high-level bid support and marketing director expertise on a 'pay-as-you-go' basis.

Winning has become a business for Denise, as a multi-award winner and professional bid writer, who has helped clients win opportunities valued at over £3.5bn. From marketing construction to chocolate, lingerie to legionella monitoring, the company Denise built has helped businesses of all types and sizes create winning marketing campaigns and successful bids.

Her love of winning started with 'slogan' competitions. Denise studied competitive behaviour as her thesis for a bachelor's degree, gaining a first; and she wrote about the impact of the internet for her Master of Arts degree, gaining a distinction. From winning TVs to mountain bikes, holidays and even two years' worth of tights, Denise understands what makes a compelling competition entry and has transferred this knowledge into winning business awards.

Having won dozens of awards herself and for clients, Denise shares her winning secrets so other business owners can gain winning recognition. Denise writes for many large companies and trains staff in bid writing. She also speaks nationally and internationally on "how to win".

Printed in Great Britain
by Amazon